The Battle of Karbala

By

Anonymous

Published by Left of Brain Books

Copyright © 2023 Left of Brain Books

ISBN 978-1-397-66917-9

First Edition

All rights reserved. No part of this publication may be reproduced, distributed, or transmitted in any form or by any means, including photocopying, recording, or other electronic or mechanical methods, without the prior written permission of the publisher, except in the case of brief quotations permitted by copyright law. Left of Brain Books is a division of Left Of Brain Onboarding Pty Ltd.

PUBLISHER'S PREFACE

About the Book

"The Battle of Karbala took place on Muharram 10, 61 AH (October 9 or 10, 680 CE) in Karbala, in present day Iraq. On one side were supporters and relatives of Muhammad's grandson Husayn ibn Ali; on the other side was a military detachment from the forces of Yazid I, the Umayyad caliph.

Husayn ibn Ali's group consisted of notable members of Muhammad's close relatives, around 72 men and women, of which some were either very old or very young. Husayn and some members of his group were accompanied by some of the women and children from their families. On the opposite side, the armed forces of Yazid I were led by Umar ibn Sa'ad and contained at least 40,000 men.

The battle field was a desert region located beside one of the branches of the Euphrates River. The battle resulted in the military defeat of Husayn ibn Ali's group, the death of almost all of his men, and the captivity of all women and children.

The Battle of Karbala is one of the most significant battles in the history of Muslims.

This battle also had significant effects on formation of subsequent revolts against the Umayyad dynasty.

The battle of Husayn ibn Ali is commemorated during an annual 10-day period held every Muharram, culminating on its tenth day, Ashura."

(Quote from wikipedia.org)

CONTENTS

PUBLISHER'S PREFACE
TRANSLATOR'S WORD 1
A BIOGRAPHY OF `ABDUL-ZAHRÁ' AL-KA`BEE (MMAUH) 5
INTRODUCTION 10
   THE FIRST PART 30
   THE SECOND PART 81

TRANSLATOR'S WORD

THIS is my humble translation for the epical story of the battle of Karbala. This is the most common story that is used to be read every year in the day of Ashurah (10th day of Moharram, the first month in islamic calendar). This story here is written directly from the available casettes with omission of the usual poems that were said in the iraqi dialect. In this book, only poems in standard Arabic were kept, and some long ones or those who were added by the narrator itself are all omitted. I tried my best on keeping the rhyme (which made me change some words positioning and/or replace words at times), but lot of them lack the rhyme and only the meaning is translated.

This story, can be really cruel to the hearing and to the eyes that read it, but this is indeed what happened back at that time in the year 61 A.H. (almost 680 A.D.). That is why shiites cry every year in this month severely. The cruelty of the enemies of the grandson of the prophet Mohammed did not even spare his infant who was carried by him on his chest, needless to say how they blocked the water from the Household of the prophet Mohammed and killed the grandson of the prophet by thirst, swords and everything their hands could bear. In this version of the story, the true cruelty even is not mentioned and only a simple picturing is gives. There are many other related stories to this battle, and this is natural because there were many resources for this battle, either from the survivors or even from the enemies themselves. Thus, there are some events that are not mentioned here, but could be mentioned in some other books that discuss this event.

In this translation, I will use the word "Allah" instead of "God" like I did in my previous translations. I believe this step makes it more closer to the Arabic culture. Here comes the guide for spelling and pronunciation:

" ' " = Simple glottal stop.
" ` " = Hard glottal stop. Foreginers usually say it like the one above, but it is a common sound in semitic languages.
"á" = Long "A" vowel, like in "Father."
"th" = Usually like "TH" in "thin."
"ð" = Like "TH" in "this."
"h" = Hard fricative sound, closer to "H" but with more voiced friction. Foreginers usually say it simply as "H"
"dh" = Hard plosive sound, usually not found in any language even semitic ones. Can be close to "D."
"zh" = Be careful here, this is NOT like "S" in "pleasure" but it is to represent an absent sound mostly in all languages which is a lighter version of the above. The representation here reflects the fact that turkish people used to spell this letter like heavy "Z."

"kh" = The usual sound in german "bach" or the scottish "loch."
"gh" = Mostly like the french R.
"q" = A hard "K" sound, like the way it is said in filippino language.
"s" = A hard "S" sound almost like "S" in "Sun" or almost like the german "ß."
"t" = A hard "T" sound, maybe closer to the japanese way of saying "T" or the spanish one.
"^" = This is a separator between letters to make sure they are not mixed into one of the combinations mentioned above.
"PUH" = Peace Upon Him/Her. Said to holy people usually.
"PUT" = Peace Upon Them.

"MADH" = May Allah Damn Him/Her. Usually said to people that are believed to damned by God for their bad deeds.

"MAPH" = May Allah Please Him/Her. Usually said to the good companions of the prophet, of the successors of the prophet, and sometimes to great scholars after they die.

"MMAUH" = May the Mercy of Allah be Upon Him/Her. Almost similar to the usual "Rest in Peace" but it is more considered like a pray to God to have the mercy upon the dead person. Usually it follows (in speech) the name of the dead person.

[...] = These are my own comments.
[C] = It means the term is coined by me.

This book, contains 4 parts. First part is a little preview over the famous narrator of this epical battle, Sheik `Abdul-Zahrá' Al-Ka`bee, whose famous voice is always in the minds of shiites all around the world. The second part is a word about the revolution of Al-Husayn (or Al-Hussein, or Al-Husain) and what were the goals and what are the benefits that Islam gained in return after such a massacre that reached the grandson of the prophet, Al-Husayn, and his companions. The third part is the story itself, and the fourth is the story of the prisoners of women and children of Al-Husayn who were captured as prisoners and their journey in captivity from Karbala in Iraq to Damascus, the capital of the Umayyad state, then back to Karbala then back to Medina.

I will try my best, and please, if you are able or trying to learn Arabic, then I advise you to read it in Arabic since the literature here is the main factor of the emotional state, especially considering the poetry that was flowing in the battle fields by the heroes of Karbala.

4

Keep a tear in your eye, you will never know when do you need it.

Taher Al-Shemaly (TJ)
Kuwait
2007

A BIOGRAPHY OF `ABDUL-ZAHRÁ' AL-KA`BEE (MMAUH)

THE evening of the 15th of the month Jamadi-Oolah (5th month of islamic calendar), 1394 A.H. was a painful evening in the city of Holy Karbala, in Iraq. At that time, the great scholar and preacher and the poet, Sheik `Abdul-Zahrá' ben Faláh Al-Ka`bee, may Allah accept him in His wide mercy and may He make him live in His wide paradise, and may He join him with the chosen prophet and the purified imams (PUT).

The 15th day of Jamadi-Oolah, 1394 A.H. was a memorable day in the holy city of Karbala in Iraq. The crowded people marched from every corner to join the funeral of the late along the long que from his house in "Hay Al-Husayn" to his grave in Al-Wádi, passing by Al-Moghtasal around the camp, (and passing by) the purified Husaynid [C] shrine, and the holy `Abbasid shrine, and some witnesses said: the procedures of his funeral were similar to those of great scholars, like putting his body in Al-`Ammári [`Ammari: something made of wood and used to put the tomb inside it as a sign of respect for the dead and it is used only for great scholars and those who are close to that level of wisdom. It is a custom used in Iran and Iraq], and the marches that went in front of the funeral.

And since the late was one of the greatest preachers in Iraq and the gulf, and since all the visitors of Al-Husayn (PUH) from all around the islamic lands used to listen to his speeches in the holy city of Karbala especially when he used to read the first part of the epical story at the 10th day of Moharram every year, and since more than one radio station used to broadcast at the 10th day of Moharram a recording with his own voice for the first part of the epical story in every year, and since more than one radio station used to broadcast at the 20th day of Safar [2nd month] of every year a recording of his own voice for the narration of the second part of the epical story, thus, many islamic lands got shocked for his death, and many newspapers and magazines wrote about his death and many mourning places were set in many cities, and I mention here for example: holy Karbala, Baghdad, Al-Samáwah, Basra, Kuwait, Beirut, Tehran and Qum.

Thus, just to give some right back to him from fellow muslims in general, and fellow shiites in special, I write here some points that elaborate some sides of the life of the late, may they become guide lines for the good faithful youth:

* His birth was at the same day of birth for the Lady of the women of the worlds, Fatima Al-Zahrá' (PUH) [the daughter of prophet Mohammed (PUH)] and for this he was called `Abdul-Zahrá' [meaning: Slave of Al-Zahrá'] and his death day was the same of her as well. This is enough as to be a coincedence of deep meanings.

* He used to sleep in one night and day, for 4 hours or 5, and that was because he was cautious to use the maximum of his life in the field of goodness.

* He was a good poet (but didn't compose much) in Arabic and in the Iraqi dialect, and he used to say what he made of poetry on the Husaynid pulpit and the listener would not recognize if this poetry was made by him or by some great poets at that time who used to say the poetry about the battle of Karbala in Arabic and the Iraqi dialect.

* He used to give most of what comes of gifts to the pulpit to the poor people in secret, and keeps the little left for himself for his life needs.

* He involved himself in an effective manner to prepare for islamic projects in all the fields, and also in establishing them, and pushing them to be continuous, so much that you wouldn't find a single islamic project in the holy city of Karbala that he didn't have any part in it.

* He took care of the young preachers until they become by time - and under the visual training and the practical work - great preachers that will call back to Allah the Exalted and the rightful path, and this is for him to help in the continuation of his preaching pupils. In recent times, Iraq, Iran and the gulf have many preachers that were took care of by him.

* He was humble to the bone, and especially to Sádah [Sádah: plural of Sayid, or Sayed. A title usually used to denote a descendant of the prophet. However, in literature it is used for other meanings], thus he used not to walk in front of a Sayid however young he might be, or humble in his social status.

* He was "Husaynid" to the bone, meaning that he was sincere about everything that is related to imam Al-Husayn (PUH). His joining to the funeral sets that was held by the people of Towaireej at the afternoon of the 10th day of Moharram in every year is a clue for this sincerity, although he was so tired at that time for working day and night in the funerals (of Al-Husayn).

* In every morning of Ashurah (the 10th day of Moharram) he used to read the story of the first part of the Husaynid Death in heart of the holy city of Karbala, which is considered a historical document for everything that happened with imam Al-Husayn and his Household and his companions and their patriotic martyrdom in the field of the battle by the hands of the ummayads. All the crowds, visiting or living there, used to gather in the markets and the streets in thousands just to listen to that story with their cries and weeping, and the radio station of Baghdad and other radio stations used to broadcast that regularly every year, and many recordings of his voice for the first part of the story were distributed all over the lands to be broadcasted at the day of Ashurah, in mosques and husayniyyas [Husayniyya or Husayniyya: A place for preaching and telling the stories of the prophet and his Household and giving lectures].

* Also, the late used to read the second part of the story, and it is what happened to the prisoners from the Household and from the companions after the killing of Al-Husayn at the 20th day of Safar in Al-Husayniyyah Al-Tahrániyyah [meaning: The Tehranic Husayniyya] that was situated in the holy city of Karbala, and the occasion was the passage of 40 days since the martyrdom of the imam. Many radio stations used to broadcast that annually. The attractiveness was close to that of narrating the first part.

* The late used to travel to the Jámi` of Kufa [Jámi`: a mosque but on a large scale] at the night of the 21st of Ramadan every year, and that was to narrate the story of the death of imam `Ali (PUH) [imam `Ali is the father of imam Al-Husayn and the husband of the prophet's daughter, Fatima] for the gathering crowds in that historical mosque, and the occasion is: the imam was praying the morning prayer in the same Jámi` at the day of the 19th of Ramadan when he received a vital hit by the hand of Ibn Moljam Al-Morádi (MADH) which caused him to die on the night of the 21st of Ramadan.

* Thus, the life of our dear late was over, and it is a bright page of directing and hard working on the way of the Household (PUT), who he used to go up the pulpit by their names and try to make himself and his listeners as examples for them. May Allah have mercy upon him when he preached and guided, and may Allah have mercy upon him when he fought (worked) and when he had the patience.

INTRODUCTION

The Goal and The Result of The Revolution of Abi-`Abdilláh Al-Husayn (PUH)

-1-

THE fight between goodness and evil is around in every society, as long as the society is a grouping of humans, among which the fight between the goodness nature and the evil nature goes on. The fight condensate inside the humans, and may be apparent on the theatre of the society in the form of a public struggle, and if the its stages and types were different according to the circumstances and the needs, however the factors and the causes that do not accept the truce and the tepidity do not change, as long as the nature of the human beings do not change, that nature which goodness and evil are clashing within it.

-2-

And since Allah made this life a place for testing and adversity, the victory was not made only for the good side over the side of evil, but the material victory was distributed evenly over the two sides, according to the level of the material capabilities and according to the merits that are derived from the material capabilities as well, even though the victory of the merits is on the side of goodness alone, always.

-3-

The ignorant society [society before Islam] was -like any society- a theatre for the fight betwen good and evil, with an exception: in the ignorant society, two main elements have grown up on each side until they mastered them, and they are the hashimite [from bani Hashim, the tribe of the prophet (PUH)] element, and the umayyad element, so was the hashimite element mastering the good side while the umayyad element was mastering the evil side, so the fight between them was natural and eternal.

Since the power of goodness was smybolized in an element until it became a secondary nature for it, and the power of evil was symbolized in another element until it became a secondary nature for it, the struggle between them was a true expression about the clash between the powers of goodness and evil.

-4-

And when the message of heaven was revealed on earth, by the appearance of Mohammed ben `Abdilláh who was in the core of the hashimite element, the merits of the hashimite element jumped to higher levels, which made it undefeatable in front of the umayyad element, or any other element of evil.

The umayyad element had no merits in its continuous fight with the hashimite element except of the internal envy of the evil elements over the elements of goodness. So, when the level of importance of the hashimite element got raised up by the message of heaven, the occasional envy joined the internal envy, and raised the merits of the umayyad, after it was fighting with the power of envy only before the revelation of the heavenly message, and after the revelation it began to fight by the power of envy and anger together.

-5-

Thus, the umayyad element was shocked by the message (of heaven), like the fighter that goes surprised by his opponent for what he never met before. The ignorant magnanimity blocked the umayyad element from holding off the silly racist fights and being humble to study the message objectively, to evaluate it and evaluate its high spirits, to know that its (the message) nature is against the defeat so it might spare itself many losses in the wars that it bore for 13 years, and not becoming a block in the arabian peninsula on the way of the wide spread of the message and be the damnation of history forever, and so it may gain the benefits of the faith, and thus the rule in this life and happiness in the Hereafter. But its nerves that got concentrated by ego, were not able to bear any logical thinking about the reality of the message or even believe in it and being under its rule. So, it (umayyad element) considered it (the message) since the time when the Messanger raised his great voice with it and forever, as the hypothesis of Mohammad ben `Abdilláh for his tribe just to gain victory for one element over the other. The repetitive calls of Quran that assures that this message is revealed from Allah to all the people equally and the Messanger was sent from Allah to be a mercy for all the people, all of that did not block its way of ego.

That was the idea of this message for the umayyad element, and by this wrong idea it decided to fight against the message, and to turn off the light of Allah on earth however that takes.

-6-

And as long as the stages that the message passed through to stabilize itself, were all resulted from each other and different from each other, according to the difference of its reasons and its material capabilities and the number of the believers that believed in it, although its core is unique, thus, the umayyad element couldn't fight it by one style only, because the style that is useful for one stage of the war is not useful for another stage of it, especially if the other side is advancing. Thus, the umayyad element changed its own ways according to the needs of each stage, but it didn't change its mentality about the message and about evaluating it, thus it continued to run the activity against the message in one mentality and by one wrong idea all over the stages.

-7-

Since the message passed through three stages to stabilize itself, the umayyad element planned for three ways to fight it, and the details of these three stages are as the following:

The first stage: the stage of the beginning of the message.. when the message was establishing its reality and its ideas that were flowing from heaven like rain drops were forming, to be connected all together and form a crawling current of a complete message, at the time that those of the conscious used to go in person or in groups to the court of the messanger near the holy Mosque (Mecca) just to see the lips of the prophet wet with inspiration and hear the phrases of Quran when it was just revealed on its way down to earth and their heart got enlightened with a light that they awaited for long time, so they believed in it one after the other. At that time when the believers were few in numbers ruled by the hand of the disbelievers, and the disbelievers were great in number and against the believers.

The style of the umayyad element in fighting the message through this stage depended on the psychological war which stood on 2 cases:

The first case: spread the rumors against the message and claim that it is a type of magic and poetry and the result of priests and crazy people's talk, and against the messanger claiming that he is a magician and a poet and also a priest and a crazy man. Also against the believers claiming that they are low down in status and got swayed away by a spell.

The second case: fighting the believers and making some of them immigrate from Mecca to Abyssinia, and making the others flee Mecca to the lands of Abu-Tálib and also making the plots against the message and the Messanger and the believers, such plots that were usually made for earthly powers like magic and poetry, and the magician and the poet and those that gets swayed away.

This style of fighting resulted in the annoyance of the prophet from Mecca and made him leave to Medina.

The second stage: The concentration of the message, when the message showed its reality and its ideas were connected and expressed a unqiue crawling message.

Since people began to get into Islam in groups and since the believers formed a strong side in front of the disbelievers, the message got concentrated by itself and based on a strong base in Medina. The messanger when left to Medina he was received by Ansár [people of Medina] with great happiness, who joined Al-Mohájireen [Arabic: the immigrants. People who immigrated from Mecca], and swore fealty to him for no conditions, thus the message gained a strategic base and that is, Medina. And a solid public base and that is Ansár and Al-Mohájireen, and an independent side which can protect its own back against any aggression and that is able to attack any side that plots against it. The prophet proved his strength in the first year after immigration (to Medina), when he blocked the way between Mecca and Shám [Syria and the surroundings], and gained control over a caravan of Qoraysh [the main tribe of Mecca] that was on the way, as soon as he acknowledged that the disbelievers are controlling the fortunes of the believers that were left in Mecca at the time of the immigration.

Here, the umayyad element found out that the psychological war which was used by them against the message in Mecca is not useless. This failure is supposed to enlighten the minds of the umayyads to look back at their previous measures which lead them to such a failure and study the message according to the lights of the previous experiments objectively away from ego and racism to measure its real powers in reality, but they never benefited from these experiments and kept fighting it with the same values that lead them to the failure, but in a different style that didn't change in the core from the experiments in Mecca, only by the amount of the difference in the situation of the message in Mecca and Medina.

Thus, in this stage, the umayyad element depended on the systematic war, so it lead wars against the message and involved in wars and encouraged other sides to fight against the message, and the umayyad element got severe losses in souls and fortunes and lost all its merits and its ego.

The third stage: the stage of the outgoing of the message... these wars and the break of the treaties that were held between the prophet and the leaders of the umayyad side, all lead to the opening of Mecca, which gave the chance to the believers to take over the bases of the disbelievers and the ratio (of power) was reversed from that which was before the immigration. Thus, the disbelievers turned out to be a minority in the hands of the disbelievers, and the believers turned to be a majority which was able to decide the destiny of the disbelievers, although the believers did meet the bad with goodness, and although the disbelievers fought the believers before the immigration, the believers had the passion over the disbelievers after the opening of Mecca, and they released all of them and treated them by the spirit of Islam which showed the message in practice in its real meanings: for all people and a mercy for the worlds, and not a hypothesis for one man to his tribe to enforce one element over another.

Here, the umayyad element knew that it can't destroy the message by weapons, but didn't realize the mistake of its general mental base in evaluating the message and measuring its real powers, so it remained measuring it by its own old measures which lead to failure twice, so now it prepared to plot for the message in a third style that was not different much from the previous two styles in the core, except the apparent difference in the situation of the message before and after the opening of Mecca.

Thus, the umayyad style in this stage depended on intrigues.

In order to achieve this style, the umayyads went under the flag of this message, as an introduction to get into the leadership, to intrigue from the inside and to falsify the message from its reality and then destroy it completely, and return it back to their rule during the age of ignorance. The prophet foretold their black intends when they entered into Islam, and foretold again about what shall be the situation of the caliphate after him, when the family of Al-`Ás [one of the umayyads] reaches 30 men, and also he assigned the duties of the believers if ever they saw Mo`áwiyah [the first umayyad ruler in the umayyad dynasty] on his pulpit.

The umayyad element went on achieving this way since the day of the opening (of Mecca), when Abu-Sufyán asked the prophet for some desires, one of these were to marry his daughter (of Abu-Sufyán) and to accept his son Mo`áwiyah as to be one of the writers of the inspiration, and so the umayyad element went on working on this for the rest of the days of the prophet, until the death of the prine of the believers (imam `Ali ben Abi-Tálib) (PUH), but the complete control for the umayyad element was not available like when it was available when Yazeed [Yazid I, second umayyad ruler] took control over the neck of muslims by the name of the caliphate, so he started establishing a wide plan to destroy the message from its heads.

The umayyad element expressed the take up of such plan in the acts and sayings of its leaders. Once `Umar [second caliph] got killed and umayyads got the chance to slip into the leadership, Abu-Sufyán announced his famous saying: catch it O umayyads like how kids catch a ball, surely I swear by whatever Abu-Sufyán swears by, there is no paradise nor hell. Mo`áwiyah also found the trust that he needs in Al-Waleed and delivered to him what was going on in his mind when he said after a long speech ... "and this is Ibn Abi Kabshah (the prophet), was not satisfied until he joined his name to the name of Allah so it is shouted with for 5 times a day on the minarets, no by Allah destroyed it shall be, no by Allah buried it shall be. And Yazeed didn't find an apparent reason to hit the basic pillar for the message and destroy its original elements unless he killed the good remain of the prophet's Household in the battle of Karbala, and then he targeted the good remains of the prophet's companion in the battle of Al-Harrah especially those who were involved in the battle of Badr [the first battle between the believers and the disbelievers after one year of immigration], and didn't spare any of them, and also spread the chaos in Medina for 3 days and it was the city of the prophet and the main base for the message by hands of his general Muslim ben `Uqbah... then when the circumstances were better for the umayyad element and no one was left to defend the message, he turned around towards Ka`bah [the holy House in Mecca] and Quran, and the holy Ka`bah was hit by catapults by `Abdul-Malik ben Marwán by the hands of his viceroy Al-Hajjáj ben Yousef Al-Thaqafi, and Al-Waleed ben `Abdul-Malik threw Quran with arrows until it was torn down.

This plan showed up in lot of statements and acts of the umayyad element.

-9-

Quran emphasized on one matter that there is no other way for it, and that is to follow the Sunna of the prophet which includes his sayings and his acts and the things that he liked, because Quran did not include all the details of the teachings that would cover the needs of all of the believers. Thus, the matters that were not covered by the Quran clearly were explained by the prophet's Sunna, thus Quran said (And whatsoever the messenger giveth you, take it. And whatsoever he forbiddeth, abstain (from it), 59:7) and this reference was explained by that the prophet doesn't decide by himself but express about Allah by the way of the inspiration, so it (the Quran) said (Nor doth he speak of (his own) desire, It is naught save an inspiration that is inspired, 53:3,4). The prophet also assured this when it came to his true successors who he gave their names. The prophet had to assure this thing about his sucessors, since not all muslims were expert in all of the laws (teachings) of the message, because of the short life of the prophet relative to the new muslims who converted into Islam in the last years of the prophet's life while people who were expert in the laws were not abundant and most of them turned to some problems that are not so much important, or never important at all. Thus, the prophet moved his wisdom to his successors who he assigned by their names and their properties and assured that people must get back to them for everything that a faithful man would not see in the reported acts (Sunna) and Quran clearly, and he explained this by that his successors do not decide by themselves but express it by the way of a direct inspiration.

Thus, the believers followed the Quran in returning back to the prophet himself and follow his Sunna as long as the Sunna is parallel to Quran in expressing (the will of) Allah. They also followed the will of the prophet about returning to his successors and following their Sunna considering it a parallel line to the original Sunna. Thus, it was natural -or more even it is a must according to the islamic order- to take every saying and every act and every satisfaction expressed by one of the prophet's successor, and be as a third source beside Quran and Sunna and explain the Quran and Sunna and enter Islam to be fixed forever beside what is fixed in Quran and Sunna.

The crowds of the belivers followed their line, and didn't recognize between whoever the prophet assigned by name and between whoever assigned himself for the caliphate.

Thus, the crowds of the believers went on with this wrong basic idea following everyone who sits on the chair of the caliphate neglecting his identity and neglecting whether the prophet named that person to be a caliph or not, and the crowds went along that way which lead to follow the ways of Mo`áwiyah and Yazeed, who lead the umayyad element, to destroy the message completely.

Imam Al-Husayn was the real successor who was assigned by the prophet (PUH) and the main person who was responsible - at his time- to protect the message, and derlivering completely to the one who follows him as he received it completely from the one who was before him. He knew this plan clearly, and he saw with his eyes plainly how the crowds were going on following the ways of Mo`áwiyah and Yazeed and claiming that by following them they are following the orders of the prophet (PUH) which suggests following his successors, and he (Al-Husayn) felt his responsibility to put down this plan and return the crowds from following the path in that way which will destroy the message and get back to the age of ignorance after Islam. So, imam Al-Husayn had to revolt not to announce that there is a mistake in the idea of the crowds about the caliph, because announcement alone is not enough in this field, but also to knock out from the feelings of the crowds of the believers the roots of the blind imitation for the ways of anyone who sits on the chair of the caliphate -either by terror and seduction or not- and to plant in the feelings of the crowds of the believers that the caliph is the one who was assigned by a command from the prophet (PUH) to follow his ways only.

The revolution had to be severe, to take over all the caliphs that took over the place of the prophet (PUH) without any rights for doing so, those caliphs that did not think about the benefits of the nation and the message but rather they thought about their own benefits, thus they applied all the capabilities of the caliphate to excuse their presence first of all, and then enforce their position. Thus, imam Al-Husayn was working to make his revolution on the level of the great goal that he was trying to achieve, so he gathered all the capabilities that can be gathered for a revolution, to make it slip through the feelings of the crowds of the believers by their minds and their emotions, and thus it would take over the ideas and the souls, and assign in the life of every single person a similar revolution that would take control of his will and change whatever of his own directions.

For this, imam Al-Husayn did not start the revolution in Medina, when Al-Waleed ben `Utbah [viceroy of Medina at that time] asked him to swear fealty, but it was enough for him to move from Medina to Mecca and remained to watch the perfect time.

-11-

Some similar feelings went through the real believers, those whose religious measures were not confused in for the confusion in the leadership, though the sacred sword and lash were the watchers over the lips for every single word that comes out against the astraying leadership.

But the weakness of Al-Nu`mán ben Basheer, the viceroy of Yazeed over Kufa, gave the chance for kufans to express their ideas away from the sacred sword and the lash, so they sent the messages to imam Al-Husayn to arrive and be their leader on the way of Allah, and take Kufa -and it is the second base of caliphate, and the destination of his father and where his father's tomb is- as a base to defame the astraying leadership.

Imam Al-Husayn knew kufans the best, since he lived many years with them and lived the experiments of his father and his brother with them, and he knew that they will betray him like how they did with his father and his brother and he knew that he would be killed if he met their request, but he answered their request because he insisted on the revolution before the kufans' invitation, he was only looking for a base for the revolution and he found it in the invitation of the kufans.

-12-

The invitation of the kufans provided a golden chance for imam Al-Husayn and it was a beneficial one for him as it was a bad one for them and imam Al-Husayn benefited from it in the following way:

1. Providing a base for the revolution. Imam Al-Husayn insisted on the revolution however it takes from him, and he announced it -by the line of events- in Medina when he refused to swear fealty to Yazeed once, and then moving from Medina to Mecca the other time. But his revolution was without a base that would make other revolutions follow it and give repetitive strikes on one target until victory is gained. Thus, the kufans invitation for imam Al-Husayn provided such a base for his revolution for it is normal that the murder of imam Al-Husayn by the hands of the kufans will spark the spirit of regret in them and make them feel their responsibility about his blood and make people blame them, thus their natural reaction would be working on clearing this bad reputation by killing his killers and spark the revolution against those who drove them to make them kill him. Such reaction indeed happened in the revolution of Al-Tawwábeen in the revolution of Al-Mokhtár and the other revolutions that made Kufa a volcano that carries the fire in its core, which whenever its top is turned down from one side, another fire would appear in another side, in another place. The fire that remained in the hearts of the kufans is the fire of regret, over murdering imam Al-Husayn.

2. Finding the dimensions of the revolution. If imam Al-Husayn was to revolt in Medina and get killed there, his revolution would have only one dimension and that is the mental dimension which is supposed to stay but only in the minds of the thinkers and it is a narrow thing even though it can affect history after such a long time but it cannot change the way of history in a wide form.

The emotional dimension was not easy to be provided in Medina, for if imam Al-Husayn was to revolt in Medina, he would be killed with his companions only and then the rumors will try to defame and misfigure this revolution until it is out of its original contents into some badly figured contents that almost have no effects in history. But the killing of innocent children or their death of thirst.. but the imprisoning of women of inspiration and those who were grown under the imamate [C], but the killing of Al-Husayn and his companions while he was supposed to be a guest who was invited and fealty was sworn for him, but killing him and his companions out of thirst beside the river, all of that was to be occuring by nature if kufans did not invite him, and these characteristics that made the revolution of Al-Husayn unique. That is, the emotional rivers that feeded his revolution to be in eternity.

Imam Al-Husayn tried to emphasize this side in his revolution by sending Muslim ben `Aqeel [Al-Husayn's cousin] before him to Kufa, to take the swear of fealty from kufans before his arrival to them.

3. Explaining the secrets of the treaty of Al-Hasan [Al-Husayn's elder brother who made a treaty with Mo`áwiyah]. Imam Al-Husayn by accepting the invitation of kufans and their treachery in that cowardly way, exposed to history some factors that were behind the treaty of Al-Hasan and his accept of the treaty instead of fighting. The treachery of kufans with imam Al-Husayn showed that if imam Al-Hasan refused the treaty he would get killed by his own companions, and that makes his murder without any further effects.

Imam Al-Husayn refused to swear the fealty to Yazeed and immigrated from Medina to Mecca and by that he announced the revolution for two times, and in Mecca he received 12 thousands invitations from kufans, and that proves that imam Al-Husayn did not refuse to swear fealty and did not immigrate to Mecca asking for the leadership and he was not swayed away by kufans, but he did what he did for his duty as a responsible for protecting the message, but he wanted to emphasize these two facts at the day when he announced in Mecca and before his travel to Kufa his knowledge about what are the developments and his intention to revolt which will end up in his martyrdom and also announced the place of his martyrdom as if he was reading a book, when he said (like I see my joints amputated by the wolves of the deserts between Al-Nawáwees and Karbala...) [Al-Nawáwees: an old village in Iraq was inhabited by christians].

-14-

Imam Al-Husayn went out giving his soul on the way of Allah, and planting patience in himself, so he got killed -like he said- and succeeded in achieving his goal, because he was able to separate the false caliphate from Islam and showed the reality of the umayyad leadership which was an ignorant leadership connecting itself to Islam as to work on turning off the light of Allah on earth, which was started at the battle of Badr.

Thus, people realized the nature of the umayyad government, as a false rule not related to Islam by any way, and has nothing to do with Islam. Thus, he saved the reality of Islam from being polluted by the crimes of the umayyad element which was considered according to the public something from Islam and should be counted by Islam.

He proved, forever, that the caliph of Allah and His prophet is not everyone who takes the throne of ruling, but it is him who was named by the prophet of Allah and assiged by him, whether he was on the throne or in the dark jails.

Under the light of the revolution of imam Al-Husayn, the reality of everyone who came after imam Al-Husayn or even before him was exposed, thus no single king from umayyads or abbasids or even ottomans could claim that his actions or statements which were illegal were part of Islam, and the islamic public did not recognize it as something from Islam and was not even claimed to be an innovation, but was considered merely like the rest of actions of kings who had no relation to religions.

-15-

The summary is: Islam has an obvious view about the caliph and that is: the caliph is whoever the prophet assigned by himself. After the prophet this measure which was emitted from the soul of Islam got confused, so everyone who took over the throne was named the caliph of Allah and His prophet. This confusion was in its extreme when Yazeed ben Mo`áwiyah became a ruler, when he became the enemy of Islam and called the caliph of Islam, thus imam Al-Husayn focused the lights of his revolution on this confusion until he destroyed it completely, and turned back the islamic public to the right measure about the islamic leadership which was expressed by the name of: the caliphate. He proved also that the sucessor of the prophet is the one who is assigned by the prophet, and whoever rules the muslims is a ruler but not a caliph, and there is a great difference between the ruler of muslims and the caliph of muslims.

-16-

Thus, the effects of the revolution of imam Al-Husayn on abbasids and ottomans were not any lesser than it was on umayyads, because it showed how false they are all together. Thus, all of them were fighting against him. Even abbasids who took the throne from the umayyads by the name of Al-Husayn started to fight Al-Husayn once they were on the throne, and if they missed him in person, they didn't miss his grave and the visitors of his grave and his descendants and his followers, and whenever a building raises up on his grave they would knock it down, and whenever a flag for the visitors of his grave would raise up they would chase them around and whenever the mention of his descendants raises up they would finish them, and whenever a voice for his followers raises up they would choke it by the sword and the lash.

-17-

The complete revolution of imam Al-Husayn is composed of two parts:

First part: his revolution itself, which exploded on the day of Ashurah and was ended by his martyrdom with all of his Household and his companions.

Second part: the capture of his women and children, and touring them in the lands, from Karbala to Kufa and from Kufa to Shám [Syria and the surroundings] and then their turn back from Shám to Karbala after 40 days, then finally going back to Medina.

The core of the revolution of imam Al-Husayn was in the first part which was took care of by the imam himself, but the second part was not controled by him but he prepared for that when he took the women and children with him over the deserts to Karbala.

The second part is considered a completion for the revolution of imam Al-Husayn from one side, and an explanation for the revolution of imam Al-Husayn on the other side.

So it was a completion for the revolution of imam Al-Husayn, because the capture of the women and the children and touring them from one land to another deepened the emotional side in the revolution, and exposed the reality of the umayyad element clearly, and made it appear like an ignorant element that steps on all the holies of Islam which it was supposed to rule by its name, and spreaded the killings and the capture of women among the descendants of the prophet of Allah which are supposed to be the true caliphs, for taking revenge for what they did to its ancestors in Badr and Hunayn.

It was also an explanation for the revolution of imam Al-Husayn, because the revolution at that time was covered with thick veils rumors that was spread by the umayyad trumpet to get it down and misfigure its reputation.

Thus, the hashimite element had to fear over its revolution and save it from the hands of the speech-falsifiers. This great part was done by imam Al-Sajjád [the only survivor son of Al-Husayn and the 4th imam for shiites. His name was "`Ali"] and his sisters and his aunts while they were captured in chains, so they announced the goal of the revolution of imam Al-Husayn and showed its features to the islamic public in a clear way away from the bad reputation and the falsification.

This book which is now between your hands -O reader- show you -in brief- the events of the revolution of imam Al-Husayn with its two parts, and it was read by the great preacher, the pious pilgrim, sheik `Abdul-Zahrá' Faláh Al-Ka`bee, in two sets that he joined in Iraq. He read the first part in a public set which was held beside the radius of imam Al-Husayn's tomb [called Al-Sahan] at the day of Ashurah in every year. He also read the second part in a public set that was held beside Al-Sahan too on Al-Arba`een [that is, the passage of 40 days after the martyrdom of Al-Husayn (PUH)] in the year 1379 A.H.

The first part is the one which is broadcasted by the radio of Baghdad on the morning of Ashurah every year since 1379 A.H. and in the same year it was broadcasted twice, once at daytime and once at night and that is because 14 thousands requests by telegrams and by phone reached the minister of culture and the station's headquarter asking to broadcast it again. It is also broadcasted in a complete form for years from the arabic radio station of Ahwáz [a town on border between Iran and Iraq] in every year at the day of Ashurah, and some parts of it are broadcasted -for two years ago- from the station of Kuwait.

The second part -which tells what happened after the death of imam Al-Husayn until his Household turned back to Medina- was broadcasted from the station of Baghdad on the morning of Al-Arba`een in the years 1379 A.H. and 1380 A.H.

The two parts are completely taken from the tapes into the papers -and the poetry that was in the local dialect was ommited because it was in the iraqi dialect, which can be hard to understand for non-iraqis- and now here it is all between your hand within this book.

Hasan Mahdi Al-Shirazi

Holy Karbala

7/2/1388 A.H. [7th of Safar]

THE FIRST PART

In the name of Allah, the Beneficent, the Merciful

WHEN Al-Husayn (PUH) got into the morning of the day of Ashurah, he stood up and preached to his companions after the noon's prayer and thanked Allah and praised Him and said: verily Allah, sanctified He is and Exalted had destined you and I to be killed in this day, so be patient and fight. Then he ranked them for the war and they were seventy seven between knights and foot soldiers and some said they were more than that. So he made Zohayr ben Al-Qayn on the right hand and Habeeb ben Mozháhir on the left hand and gave his banner to his brother Al-`Abbás (PUH) [the brother of Al-Husayn but from a different mother] and he remained (PUH) with his Household in the heart. They made the tents at their backs and he ordered to bring some wood and sticks to be put behind the tents in a trench that they have made there at some time at night and ordered to set fire to it so that to avoid attacks from the back and it was useful for them.

Then, `Umar ben Sa`d marched towards Al-Husayn ben `Ali (PUT) (with at least 30,000) and he put on the right hand `Amr ben Al-Hajjáj Al-Zobaydi, and on the left hand Shimr ben Ðil-Jawshan, and head of the knights was `Urwah ben Qays and the head over the foot soldiers was Shabth ben Rab`ee and the banner was with his slave Dorayd, and they all came besieging the tents and saw the fire in the trench, and then Shimr called: O Husayn, you hurried on to the fire before the judgement day? Al-Husayn then said: who is that, seems like it is Shimr, and they answered him yes!! He then replied: O son of the goat shepherdess you are better for being burnt with it.

Then Muslim ben `Awsajah wanted to shoot an arrow at him but Al-Husayn ordered him not to and said: I hate to start the battle, and when Al-Husayn looked at their crowds like the raging flood he raised his hands for praying and said:

Allahoma [O my Lord] Thou art my trust in every adversity, and my hope in every trial, and Thou art for me in every matter a trust and a support. How many adversity weakens the core and lessens the plans and in which the friend lets down and the enemy turns happy for it I would rely (for it) on Thee and complained about it to Thee for my desire to Thee among all of the others, and Thou hath made it easy for me. Thou art the Owner of every favor and the Owner of every reward and the end of every desire. Then he asked for his camel and he rode it and called with a loud voice and most of them heard it, and he said: O people listen to my speech and don't be in a hurry until I preach for you for what is your right upon me and until I apologise for my arrival to you, thus if you accepted my apology and believed in my speech and gave me my rights you shall be happier with that and then you would have no reasons against me, and if you didn't accept my apology and didn't give the rights then gather up with your partners and don't let your matter be a cloudy one over you and then tell me what did you decide, and my support is Allah who revealed the book and He cares for the faithful.

When the women heard that from him they shouted and cried out loud and their voices raised up, so he sent to them his brother Al-`Abbás and his son `Ali and said to them: make them go silent, by my life their cries shall be more, and when they went silent, he thanked Allah and praised Him and blessed

Mohammed and his Household and said the peace over the angels and the prophets and said so many uncountable things, and no speaker before him or after him was heard with such eloquence:

He who brought the eloquent speech is a reporter
from them or otherwise he steals
They were made equals for the book of Allah
although it is silent and they are the book that speaks

Then he said: Thank be to Allah who created life and made it a home of vanishing and extinction, controling its people from one situation to another, and the proud is the one who was deceived by it and the wretched is the one who got swayed with it, so do not be deceived by this life because it cuts the hopes of those who take refuge in it and disappoint the greed of those who wish for it. I see you and you've gathered for something that Allah turned angry with you for it and turned His glorious Face away from you and revealed His wrath upon you and avoided you from His mercy. Thus, praised He is our God and evil is what bondmen are you. You've swore fealty and obedience and believed in the messanger Mohammed (PUH) and then you've crawled towards his descendants and his Household desiring their killing. Verily the devil had taken over you and made you forget to mention the name of Allah the Great, so woe to you and to what you are asking for. We are to Allah and we shall turn back to Him. These are people that disbelieved after their believing and a far removal for wrong-doing folk! Then he said: and then, retrace my ancestry and see who am I, and then turn back to yourselves and blame yourselves and see are you allowed to kill me and violate my own property. Am I not the son of the daughter of your own prophet and the son of his successor and his cousin and (the son of) the first one who believed in the messanger of Allah for what he had brought from his God, is not Hamzah the master of martyrs is my father's uncle? Is not Ja`far Al-Tayyár who is in paradise with two wings is my uncle? Did you not hear what the prophet (PUH) said about me and my brother "these are the masters of youth of paradise," so if you believed me in what I am saying and it is the truth, by Allah then I didn't lie for a purpose since I knew that Allah hate liars, and if you didn't believe in me there are people among you whom if you asked shall tell you about this matter. Ask Jábir ben `Abdullah Al-Ansári and Abá Sa`eed Al-Khidri and Sahl ben Sa`d Al-Sá`idi and Zayd ben Arqam and Anas ben Málik and Al-Borá' ben `Ázib, they shall tell you that they heard such speech from the prophet (PUH) about me and my brother, shall not this avoid you from killing me? Then Shimr ben Ðil-Jawshan said to him: he is a true worshipper who understood what you are saying, and then Habeeb ben Mozháhir replied back at him and said: by Allah I see you worship Allah for seventy folds and I testify that you are saying the truth, you don't know what he (Al-Husayn) is saying because Allah had blackened your heart.

Then Al-Husayn (PUH) said to them: if you are in doubt about that, do you doubt that I am the son of the daughter of your prophet? By Allah there is no son of daughter of a prophet like me in between the east and west and no one in others other than you. Woe to you, are you after me for a victim that I've killed? Or a fortune of you that I've used? Or for a revenge for some injury that I've made? But no one answered him.

Then he called: O Shabth ben Rab`ee, O Hajjár ben Abjar, O Qays ben Al-Ash`ath, O Zayd ben Al-Hárith, didn't you all write to me that the fruit had ripened and the fields turned green, and if you come you shall find soldiers that are made for you?

They said: we did not! He (PUH) said then: Sanctified is Allah! Yes by Allah you did, then he said: O people, if you hate me then let me leave to my safe place on the lands.

Then Qays ben Al-Ash`ath said to him: don't you come down under the rule of your cousin? [meaning Yazeed] They will show you only what you like and never hurt you, then Al-Husayn said to him: you are the brother of your own brother, do you want the hashimites to ask after more than the blood of Muslim ben `Aqeel, no by Allah, I shall not give you my hand like a humble and shall not run away like a slave. O bondmen of Allah, I have sought refuge in my Lord and your Lord lest ye stone me to death, I seek refuge in my Lord and your Lord from every scorner who believeth not in a Day of Reckoning. Then he kneeled down his camel and ordered `Uqbah ben Sam`án to tie it:

I did not forget him when he preached to them
while they have no words to say
Calling am I not the son of the daughter of your prophet
and your refuge if the life went to astray
Did I make some innovations in the religion of the prophet
or was I in doubt of what its laws say
Did not the prophet advise for us by his will
and left among you the Household and the book's way
If you did not believe in the judgement day
then turn back to your ancestry if you were arabs I say
And they turned away puzzled and see nothing
for his preach except the spears and arrows replying the say

And then the crowds started to crawl towards him. Among them there was `Abdullah ben Hawzah Al-Tamimi who shouted and said: is Al-Husayn among you? In the third [seems he shouted 3 times] the companions of Al-Husayn replied back and said: this is Al-Husayn what do you want? He said: O Husayn I bring you the tidings of hell, and Al-Husayn said: you lied, but I shall come forward before a forgiving and obeyed God, who are you? He said: Ibn Hawzah, then Al-Husayn (PUH) raised his hands high until the whiteness of his armpit showed up and said: Allahoma [O my Lord] take him to the hell! Then Ibn Hawzah turned angry and rode the horse towards him while there was a stream between them, but his leg got hanged on the stirrup and the horse toured him in that way until he fell down from the horse and his leg was amputated along with his ankle and his thigh and his other half remained hanged with the stirrup and the horse knocked his body with every tree and every stone until he died. Masrooq ben Wá'il Al-Hadhrami said: I was at the head of the horses that went to fight Al-Husayn for I was wishing for the head of Al-Husayn and thus I might catch a fortune from Ibn Ziyád [the viceroy of Yazeed over Kufa] and when I saw what happened to Ibn Hawzah I realized that the Household had a great honor and a great place by Allah, and then I left the people and said (to myself): I shall not fight them and become in hell!

Then Zohayr ben Al-Qayn went out for them on a horse with his weapon and he said: O people of Kufa, this is a warning for you against the wrath of Allah. This is a warning that a muslim has the right of advice over his muslim brother, and we are with you still on one religion as long as the sword did not fall in between us, and you are deserving for the advice and when the sword falls down, thus the bondage will be cut and we shall be a nation and you shall be another nation. Allah had verily tested us with the Household of His prophet Mohammed (PUH) to see what we and you shall do about them. We are calling you to be victorious to them, and to let down the tyrant Yazeed and `Ubaydilláh ben Ziyád for you do not realize from them except of their bad rule, to take out your eyes and amputate your hands and legs and cut you into pieces and raise you up over the palms and kill people like you and the best of you who could read (Quran) like Hijr ben `Adiy and his companions and Háni ben `Urwah and his likes!! Then they cursed him and praised `Ubaydilláh ben Ziyád and prayed for him and said: we shall not leave until we kill your partner (Al-Husayn) and whoever was with him or we shall send him with his companions to `Ubaydilláh ben Ziyád in peace!!

Then Zohayr ben Al-Qayn said: O bondmen of Allah, the son of Fatima deserves loyalty and to be victorious for more than the son of Somayyah [Yazeed], and if you are not willing to be victorious for them then I shall take refuge by Allah not to kill them, so leave this man and Yazeed for by my life he (Yazeed) accepts your obedience without killing Al-Husayn (PUH).

Then Shimr shot an arrow at him and said: shut up, my Allah shut off your voice! You've bored us with your so much talking, then Zohayr said: O son of him who pisses on his heels I am not talking to you, you are but a beast! by Allah, I don't think you are able to acknowledge two phrases from the book of Allah (Quran) so be glad with the shame on the judgement day and the harsh punishment, then Shimr said: Allah shall kill you with your partner (Al-Husayn) after some time, then Zohayr said: are you scaring me with death? By Allah, dying with him is more beloved to me than being eternal with you, then he went towards the crowds and said in a loud voice: O bond men of Allah, don't let this harsh man his likes make you astray from your religion, by Allah, a nation that spread the blood of the Household of Mohammed and his descendants and killed their companions and those who protect their harem will never receive the intercession of Mohammed.

Then a man from the companions of Al-Husayn called him and said: Abá `Abdilláh (Al-Husayn) say to you: come back, for by my life, if the believer man of the Pharaoh's family advised his people and prayed much, then you've advised those people. [The believer man of the Pharaoh's family is a story mentioned in Quran about a faithful man who believed in Moses and was among the Pharaoh's family and maybe his minister]

Then Borayr ben Khodhayr asked for a permission from Al-Husayn to talk to the people and he allowed him, and he was a faithful old man and a reader of Quran and one of the sheiks of Kufa and was a noble man among the (tribe of) hamadanites.

So he stopped near them and called: O people, verily Allah sent Mohammed with good tidings and warnings and a caller for Allah by His permission and an enlightening light, and this is the water of Al-Forát (Euphrates) which is open to the black boars and dogs but blocked away from the son of the propht of Allah, is that the reward of Mohammed? They replied: O Borayr, you've talked too much so stop it, by Allah Al-Husayn shall get thirsty like those who were before him!

He said: O people, the heaviness of Mohammed is now over your backs, and these are his Household and descendants and his daughters and harem, so show what do you have and what do you want to do with them?

They said: we want to force them down to the prince `Ubaydilláh ben Ziyád so that he decides about them. He replied: don't you accept for them to return back to where they came from? Woe to you! O people of Kufa did you forget your letters and covenants that you've sent and made Allah a witness over them? Woe to you! did you invite the Household of your prophet and claimed that you would kill yourselves for them and when they arrive at you, you give them to Ibn Ziyád and blocked their way to Al-Forát? Evil is what you've done with the Household of your prophet! What happened to you? May Allah never make you drink on the judgement day, evil is the kind of people you are. Then some of them said: O man, we don't understand what you are saying, and he replied: thank be to Allah who increased in my insight among you, Allahoma [O my Lord] verily I make myself clear from the deeds of those people! Allahoma throw the arrows among them until they meet You and You angry with them.

Then the people started to shoot arrows at Borayr and he stepped back, and then Al-Husayn rode his horse and took the Quran and put over his head and stood in front of the crowds and shouted out loud: by Allah do you know me? They said: yes, you are the son of the daughter of the prophet and his grandson, then he said: by Allah, do you that my grandfather is the prophet of Allah? They said: yes. He said: by Allah, do you know that my father is `Ali ben Abi-Tálib (PUH)? They said: yes, he said then: by Allah, do you know that my mother is Fatima the daughter of the prophet of Allah? They said: yes, then he said: by Allah, do you know that my grandmother is Khadeejah bent Khowaylid [the mother of Fatima who was a noble woman as well in Mecca] the first woman to become a muslim in this nation? They replied: yes, then he said: by Allah, do you know that Hamzah the master of martyrs is my father's uncle? They replied: yes, then he said: by Allah, do you know that Ja`far Al-Tayyár in paradise is my uncle? They said: yes, then he said: by Allah, do you know that this is the sword of the prophet of Allah that I'm holding in my hand? They said: yes, then he said: by Allah, do you know that this is the turban of the prophet of Allah that I am wearing? They replied: yes, then he said: by Allah, do you know that `Ali [his father] was the first man in this nation to become a muslim and the most wise of all and the greatest with patience and he is the viceroy over every believer? They said: yes, then he said: then why are you running to kill me? And my father is the protector, and the banner shall be in the hands of my father in the day of judgement, they said:

we knew all of that and we shall never leave you until you die out of thirst.

In a narration, that he (PUH) rode over his camel and went out to the crowds and asked them to listen by they denied to do so, until he said to them: woe to you, why don't you listen to me and I am calling you to the rightful path and whoever obeyed me shall be guided and whoever disobeyed me shall be doomed and all of you will disobey my orders and would never listen to me, and that is because your abdomens are full of the taboo and your hearts were blackened, woe to you don't you listen, and then the companions of `Umar ben Sa`d blamed each other and then they said: listen to him.

Then he (PUH) praised Allah and blessed Mohammed and the angels and the prophets and extended with his eloquent speech and then he said: woe to you O people when you called for us with urge and we came to you in a hurry, you've raised a sword upon us that was for us and kept a fire that we kept for our enemy and yours and thus you've became united with your enemies against your rulers for no justice that they might have spread among you nor for a hope that was made for you within them, except of the taboo in this life that they will give you and a low living that you've been greedy for, for nothing that we've done and no opinion was offered. Did you like the woes? You left us and the swords are raised and the self is feeling safe, and the opinion should be for the wise, but you went in a hurry for it and came to it like the butterflies, then woe to you O slaves of this nation and the strangers of the parties and haters of the (holy) book and falsifiers of the speeches, you gangs of sins and the breath of the devil and the turners of the Sunna and killers of the children of the prophets and the terminators of the Households of the viceroys and followers of the adulterers in their lineage, and you who hurt the believers and the screams of the scoffers, those who break the Quran into parts, and woe to them for what their souls commited and in the hell they shall be eternal. Woe to you! Do you nourish those? and let us down? Yes by Allah, it is an old habit of you (to betray)! and your lineages have grown with that and your descendants took it over, and your hearts grown stable with it and your chests were blackened, thus you've become the most evil fruit that ripened and an easy food for the aggressor, may Allah damned the betrayers who break the covenant after the agreement and you've made Allah a witness over you, by Allah yes you are (like that)! The bastard, the son of the bastard [meaning Ibn Ziyád] had chosen two, either to fight or to humiliate, and far it would be for us to be humiliated, for Allah fobids this for us as well as His prophet and the believers, and the kind ancestry (of us) and the purified laps (who bore us) and dignified noses and the free souls, all deny this for us and to like to follow the mean rather than die with dignity.

Verily, I've warned you. Verily, I shall go on with this family with the few numbers and the numbered enemies and without nourishers, and then he said those lines of poetry for Farwah ben Mosayk Al-Morádi:

If we are defeated, we are the victorious in advance
and if we are taken over we are not of defeats
Verily we are not satisfied with cowardice
but it is our deaths and the state of others
If the death is taken away from some people
verily then it will settle on some others
And that vanished the trees of my people
as it vanished as well the old centuries
Thus if the kings were eternal we shall be too
and if they remained alive we would have long lives
Then say to those malevolents, stay awake
verily the malevolents will face like we did face

Then by Allah, you shall not remain after this for long and once you ride the horses until it (the life) shall turn around with you like the stone handmill and turned around on you, this is a covenant that my father made to me as well as my grandfather (the prophet) made it to him, then gather up your partners and deicde, and don't let it a clouded matter for you, and tell me what did you decide.

Verily, I've depended on Allah, my God and your God, no single living creature unless He shall take it back, verily my God is on a straight path. Then he raised his hands and said: Allahoma, catch away from them the drops of the heavens, and send over them some years like the years of Joseph and make the kid of Thaqeef rule over them [meaning Al-Mokhtár who revenged for Al-Husayn] and make them drink from a bitter cup, who shall not leave one of them unless he would kill him with one type (of killing) and hit him with one type (of hitting) who shall take revenge for me and for my companions and my Household and my followers from them, for they tricked us and lied to us and let us down, and You are our Lord, we've depended on You, and to You shall end the destiny.

Then Al-Husayn (PUH) called for `Umar ben Sa`d, and they called him to the meeting and he hated to come and meet him, and then he said: O `Umar, you will kill me and you claim that the bastard, the son of the bastard will give you the rule of Al-Ray and Jorján? [areas in Iran] By Allah, you shall be happy with that at all, it is a covenant that was made, do whatever you want to do, you shall not be happy in this life or the Hereafter, as if I see your head being on a stick that stands in Kufa and the kids shall play with it. Then, `Umar ben Sa`d turned his face away with anger and then he called his companions and said:

what are you waiting for? Fight all together at once it is but only one bite.

When Al-Hur ben Yazeed Al-Riyáhee [the man who blocked the way of Al-Husayn and delivered him into Karbala] saw that the crowds insisted on fighting A-Husayn (PUH), he said to `Umar ben Sa`d: will you fight this man? He replied: yes by Allah, a fight in which at least the heads would fall down with the hands! He (Al-Hur) said then: aren't you satisfied with what he offered? He replied: if it was in my hands I would be (satisfied), but your prince [Ibn Ziyád] denied that. Then Al-Hur left him and he advanced in front of the crowds with a man from his tribe called Qorrah ben Qays, and he said (to him): O Qorrah, did you water your horse today? He replied: no I didn't, then he said: don't you want to water him? Qorrah said: by Allah, I thought he wanted to stay from the battle and the fight, and didn't want me to see that if he did, so I said to him: I didn't water my horse and I shall go to water it, and I left that place in which he was, and by Allah if he showed me what he desired then I would go out with him to Al-Husayn (PUH). Then Al-Hur began to approach towards Al-Husayn a little by little, and then Al-Mohájir ben Aws said to him: what do you want O son of Yazeed? Do you want to fight? But he didn't answer and his body started to shake, and Al-Mohájir then said to him: your situation is doubtful, by Allah I've never saw you like that before and if I was asked who is the bravest among the people of Kufa I wouldn't choose anyone but you! So what is that that I see from you? Then Al-Hur: by Allah, verily I'm giving the options for myself to choose between paradise and te hell, and by Allah I shall not choose anything but the paradise, even if I was to be cut into pieces and burnt.

Then he struck his horse towards Al-Husayn (PUH) and put his hand over his head and said: Allahoma to You I go, have mercy upon me for I scared the hearts of Your viceroys and the children of Your own prophet (PUH), and then he said to Al-Husayn (PUH): may I be a ransom for you O son of the prophet of Allah, I am the one who kept you away from turning back and marched with you all the way and made you settle in this land, and I don't think the crowds will answer your offer and never reach closer to you, by Allah if I knew they are planning to do this, I wouldn't have done what I've done already, and here I am I've came to you to repent to my Lord for what I did, and sacrficing myself for you until I die between your hands, so do you see any forgiving for me? Then Al-Husayn (PUH) said: yes, Allah shall forgive you so come down, but he replied: I am better for you on my horse rather than on my foot, and I shall fight them over my horse for some time and then at the end I shall come down, so then Al-Husayn to him: do whatever you see may Allah have mercy upon you. Then he stepped in front of Al-Husayn and said: O people of Kufa, did you invite this faithful man and when he arrived you tried to capture him, and you claimed that you are willing to kill yourselves to protect him and then stepped with aggression towards him to kill him, and imprisoned him and surrounded him from all the sides to keep him away from going on the wide lands of Allah, so he became like the hostage between your hands and has no power for himself and blocked his away with his women and children and his family from the water of Al-Forát which goes on and jews with christians and the magians drink from it as well as the black boars and the dogs roll in it, and here are they killed by the thirst, evil is what you've done to the Household of Mohammed after him, may Allah never make you drink when you become thirsty. Then some men shot arrows on him so he stepped back until he stood in front of Al-Husayn (PUH) and then said to Al-Husayn (PUH): if I was the first one to come out to fight you, then let me be the first one to get killed before your hands, may I be one of those who shall shake the hands with your grandfather Mohammed (PUH) tomorrow in the judgement day, so Al-

Husayn (PUH) gave him the permission, and he attacked the fellows of `Umar ben Sa`d while saying:

Verily I am Al-Hur the safe place of the guest
and I shall strike your necks with the sword
Defending the purest who stepped on Al-Khayf [spot in Mecca]
I shall strike you and see no lesser to this word

Then he fought severely until he killed around 40 men of them, and he was attacking with Zohayr ben Al-Qayn, thus whenever one man attacks and went deep inside them, the other would attack to rescue his partner. Then the foot soldiers attacked Al-Hur and surrounded him in great numbers until they killed him, and the companions of Al-Husayn (PUH) carried his body until they put it between the hands of Al-Huysan (PUH) while his soul still not released and his blood was gushing out, and Al-Husayn (PUH) rubbed the dust off his face and said: Bakhen Bakhen [expression to congratulate] for you O Hur, you are Al-Hur like your mother named you, you are free in this life and the Hereafter. [Hur means "the free man" or "free" in Arabic].

Then `Umar ben Sa`d stepped towards the camp of Al-Husayn (PUH) and put an arrow in his bow and shot at the camp and said: testify for me at the court of the prince that I am the first to shoot, and then the crowds started to shoot and the arrows arrived from the crowds like the rain and no single companion of Al-Husayn was spared, and then Al-Husayn (PUH) said to his companions: stand up may the mercy of Allah befall upon you, to the death that is awaiting, for these arrows are the messages of the crowds to you.

There was among the fellows of Ibn Sa`d [`Umar] a man called Yazeed ben Al-Mohájir Al-Kindi and his title was Abul-Sha`thá', and when the crowds replied back at the offer of Al-Husayn

(PUH) he went to his camp and fought between his hands while saying:

I am Yazeed and my father is Al-Mohájir
braver than a lion in his own lair
O my Lord I am a nourisher for Al-Husayn
and for Ibn Sa`d I shall leave forever

then he sat down before Al-Husayn (PUH) and shot 100 arrows and 5 hit the target, and every time he shot an arrow Al-Husayn used to say to him: Allahoma, make his shot in the target and let his reward be the paradise, so he killed 5 of the fellows of `Umar ben Sa`d with his arrows and he was the first to kill.

Then the crowds battled and fought for some time and when the dust was cleared out, they found 50 companions of Al-Husayn dead, then Al-Husayn (PUH) held his beard with his hand and said: Allah got angry over the jews for they made up a son for Him, and got angry over the christians for they made Him the third of three, and got angry over the magians for worshipping the sun and the moon instead of Him, and got angry over some people that agreed to kill the son of the daughter of their prophet. By Allah, I shall not answer them for what they desire until I meet Allah the Exalted painted with my blood.

Then Yasár the slave of Ziyád showed up, and Sálim the slave of `Ubaydilláh ben Ziyád as well and they said: who shall combat, and then Habeeb ben Mozháhir and Borayr ben Khodhayr stood up, but Al-Husayn (PUH) said to them: sit down, and then `Abdulláh ben `Umayr Al-Kalbi stood up and took the permission from Al-Husayn (PUH) to combat with them, and he was a tall man with wide shoulders, and Al-Husayn (PUH) looked at him and said: verily I think he is a killer of people of his likes, and he gave him the permission (and he went out of Kufa at night with his wife Um-Wahab for Al-Husayn (PUH) because when he saw the soldiers among the palm trees going to fight Al-Husayn (PUH), he said then: by Allah I am cautious to fight the disbelievers and I hope that fighting those people that are going to fight the son of the daughter of their prophet is not any less in rewards from that fighting with the disbelievers, and he told his wife about it and she said: you are right, go out and let me go out with you).

Then when he went out, Yasár faced him and said to him: who are you? So he mentioned for him his lineage and ancestry [a habit of Arabs in combat to mention the ancestry of each side before fighting], then he said to him: I don't know you, let Zohayr ben Al-Qayn get out for me or let Habeeb ben Mozháhir or Borayr ben Khodhayr, and then Ibn `Umayr [`Abdulláh] said: O son of the adulteress, are you afraid to face some people in a combat? No one goes out to combat with you unless he is better than you. Then he (`Abdullah) went down on him with his sword and while he was busy with him (with Yasár), Sálim attacked him as well and his companions shouted out loud: the slave is attacking you, but he didn't care about it and then Sálim went down with his sword on him but he received it with his hand and his fingers were amputated and then Ibn `Umayr attacked him until he killed him so got back (to the camp) and he killed both of them while he was saying:

If you deny me then I tell you I am the son of Ibn Kalb
the lineage of my ancestry is with He who knows the ancestry
I am someone of bitterness and sharp (like a sword)
and not a coward at the time of the adversity
I am promising you O Um-Wahab
to stab them truely and beat them as well accordingly

Then Um-Wahab his wife took a pillar and went towards him and said to him: may my father and mother be a ransom for you, fight for the sake of the purified, the Household of Mohammed (PUH), and he wanted to get her back to the tent but she didn't go along with him and started to hold his clothes and said: I shall not leave you until I die with you, and then Al-Husayn called her and said: may you be rewarded from the Household of your prophet with goodness, get back to the tent for women are not supposed to fight, and so she got back.

Then `Abdulláh ben `Umayr fought bitterly until he killed another two, and then he was killed by Háni ben Thobayt Al-Hadhrami and Bakeer ben Hay Al-Tamimi.

Then `Umar ben Khálid Al-Saydáwi stood up to fight and then Al-Husayn (PUH) said to him: advance, we shall be after you after some time, then he fought with his slave Sa`d and with Jábir ben Al-Hárith Al-Salmáni and Majma` ben `Abdulláh Al-`Á'iði and all of them attacked the crowds of Kufa, and when they went deep inside them, they turned around them and blocked them away from their partners, and then Al-Husayn (PUH) sent to them his brother Al-`Abbás and he saved them by his sword, and they were all injured, and on the way back the enemy approached them so they raised their swords with all the injuries they had and fought until they all got killed in one place.

Then when the companions of Al-Husayn (PUH) looked at how much men they lost, men started to take permissions from Al-Husayn to protect him and defend the harem in groups, while they protect each other from the attacks of the enemy. Thus, two young men came to him and they are: Sayf ben Al-Hárith ben Saree` and Málik ben `Abdulláh ben Saree` and they were cousins and brothers from the mother side, and they took the permission from him to fight before him, and Al-Husayn (PUH) allowed them to, and they fought bitterly until they got killed.

And then the two Ghafáris [their tribe name is Al-Ghafári], and they are: `Abdulláh and `Abdul-Rahmán the sons of `Urwah and they said to Al-Husayn (PUH): peace upon you O Abá-`Abdilláh, we've come to fight before you and defend you, and he said: welcome, and then he asked them to get closer to him, and so they did while they were crying, and he said: what makes you cry O children of my brother? By Allah, I hope you shall be satisfied and happy after some time from now, and they said: may Allah make us a ransom for you, we are not crying for ourselves but we are crying for you, we see you surrounded by enemies and we cannot help you, so he said then: may Allah reward you O children of my brother for your sacrifice with goodness as best as it can be, then they stepped forward and said: peace upon you O son of the prophet of Allah, and then he said: and peace upon you (two) and the mercy of Allah and His blessings, and then they fought close by until they got killed.

Then Al-Husayn (PUH) shouted out loud: aren't there any helper that would help us for the sake of Allah, aren't there any defender that would defend the house of the prophet of Allah, and the women and children heard him and started to scream out loud.

Then, Sa`d ben Al-Hárth Al-Ansári Al-`Ajaláni and his brother Abul-Hotoof heard the call of Al-Husayn (PUH) and the screams of his children and they were with `Umar ben Sa`d, so they raised their swords with Al-Husayn against his enemies and started to fight until they killed some men and injured some others until they got killed together.

Then, the companions of Al-Husayn when they became less in number and their shortage of men began to show up, man after another started to show up and fight, and they killed so many of the kufans.

Then, `Amr ben Al-Hajjáj shouted at his companions and said: do you know who are you fighting? you are fighting the knights of the land and the people of the insight and people that don't care about death! No one would go out to fight with them unless he got killed although they are just a few, by Allah if you don't stone them you won't kill them.

Then, `Umar ben Sa`d said: the truth you've said! The opinion is what you've said, so send the orders to the crowd not a single a man shall fight with them for if you go on in singles for sure they will terminate you.

Then, `Amr ben Al-Hajjáj attacked the right wing of Al-Husayn (PUH) but they were stable against him and they kneeled down and raised the spears so the horses couldn't advance, and when the horses went to get back, the companions of Al-Husayn shot the arrows at them, so they killed some of them and injured some others. Then `Amr ben Al-Hajjáj attacked from the direction of Al-Forát and they fought for some time, and there where Muslim ben `Awsajah Al-Asdi fought, and attacked them Muslim ben `Abdilláh Al-Dhabábi and `Abdulláh Al-Bajali, and the heavy dust turned into the air from the fierce battle, and when it was cleared out they found Muslim ben `Awsajah on the ground with some life in him. So, Al-Husayn walked to him with Habeeb ben Mozháhir Al-Asdi, and Al-Husayn said to him: may Allah have mercy upon you O Muslim! Some of them have paid their vow by death (in battle), and some of them still are waiting; and they have not altered in the least, and then Habeeb got closer to him and said: your death is hard for me! O Muslim be glad in paradise! Then Muslim said in a faint voice: may Allah bring the good tidings to you. Then Habeeb said to him: if I wasn't sure that I will be after you in few moments, I would like to ask you to recommend for me whatever you like, then Muslim replied: verily, I recommend this for you, and he pointed to Al-Husayn (PUH) so fight before him until you die. Then Habeeb said to him: verily I shall make you glad! Then he died may Allah be pleased with him.

They nourished you alive and also when they were dead
each partner recommend for the other to nourish you
Ibn `Awsajah recommended to Habeeb and said
fight before him until the fierce death comes after you

Then a maid for him (`Awsajah) shouted: Alas! my master! Alas! Ibn `Awsajah! Then the companions of Ibn Sa`d shouted in happiness: we've killed Muslim ben `Awsajah, and then Shabth ben Rab`ee said: may your mothers bereave you, verily you are killing yourselves by your own hands and humiliate yourselves for the others, are you glad that you killed Muslim ben `Awsajah? By the One that I've been muslim for, how many good deeds he had among the muslims, and I saw him at the day of Azerbaijan killing 6 disbelievers before the horses of the muslims are cured.

Then, Shimr ben Ðil-Jawshan attacked with his companions on the companions of Al-Husayn (PUH), and Zohayr ben Al-Qayn attacked them back with 10 men from the companions of Al-Husayn (PUH) so they made them stay away from the tents and they killed Abá `Aðrah Al-Dhabábi, one of the companions of Shimr, and then Shimr turned around on them so they killed some of them and the rest turned back to their positions, and Abu-Thomámah Al-Sá'idi [or Al-Saydáwi] killed one of his cousins who was an enemy of his.

Then, the time of the noon's prayer arrived, and Abu-Thomámah Al-Saydáwi said to Al-Husayn (PUH): O Abá

`Abdilláh, myself for yourself to be a ransom, these got closer to you and by Allah you shall not be killed until I die before you and I like to meet Allah after praying this prayer. Then Al-Husayn (PUH) raised his head into the sky and said: you've remembered the prayer time may Allah make you one of the prayers and the sanctifiers, yes this is the beginning of its time, and then he said: ask them to stop so that we can pray, and so they did. Then Al-Hosayn ben Tameem said to them: it shall not be accepted [meaning the prayer shall not be accepted before Allah].

Then Habeeb ben Mozháhir said to him: you've claimed that the prayer is not accepted from the Household of the prophet (PUH) and their nourishers and shall be accepted from you O jackass? Then Al-Hosayn attacked him and Habeeb attacked as well and he struck the face of his horse with the sword and Al-Hosayn fell down, and shouted for help from his companions and so they did and they attacked Habeeb and he killed one man of them.

Then, Al-Husayn (PUH) said to Zohayr ben Al-Qayn and Sa`eed ben `Abilláh Al-Hanafi: stand in front of me to let me pray the noon's prayer, and so they did with half of the companions until he prayed the prayer of Fear, then one arrow reached Al-Husayn (PUH) and Sa`eed ben `Abdilláh stood to protect him against the arrows by his body and he remained like that while arrows kept on coming to him until he fell down on the ground and said: Allahoma, damn them like the damnations of `Ád and Thamood, Allahoma, tell Your prophet the peace from me and tell him what I saw of painful injuries, for verily I wanted Your reward for protecting the Household of Mohammed (and in some other narrations he said: Allahoma, nothing of what You desire is impossible for You, so tell Mohammed (PUH) how I nourished and protected Al-Husayn (PUH) and make me be with him in the eternity). Then he died, may Allah be pleased with him, and they found out 13 arrows planted in his body, adding to that the strikes of swords and spears. Then, Sowayd ben `Amr ben Abi-Motá` advanced and he was a noble and a faithful man of many prayers, and he said:

Defend Al-Husayn today and you shall meet Mohammed
and your lord `Ali, the man of the virtues
And Hasan like the moon in its full shape
and your uncle the eager for flesh and the pious
Hamzah the lion of Allah verily called the lion
and the one with the one of two wings got place so glorious
in the paradise going there in the high places
[one of two wings is Jafar the uncle of Al-Husayn]

So he fought like the brave lion and had the great patience over the adversities until he fell down with the dead with so many injuries, and he remained like that without any movement until he heard them later on saying that Al-Husayn (PUH) got killed so he carried himself hardly and got a knife out of his sandal and fought until he got killed, may Allah be pleased with him.

Then, Zohayr ben Al-Qayn got out saying:

Verily I am Zohayr and I am the son of Al-Qayn
I shall fight you with the sword to defend Al-Husayn
Verily Al-Husayn is one of the Grandsons [of the prophet]
from the Household of the virtuous and the most fine
Verily that is the prophet of Allah
and I shall strike you and see no harm within
O how I wish my soul would be splitting

Then he fought fiercely until he killed as some narrations go, 120 men, and then he was attacked by `Abdulláh Al-Tamimi and Mohájir ben Aws Al-Tamimi and they killed him. Then Al-Husayn

(PUH) said when Zohayr got killed: may Allah not make you far away O Zohayr and may He damn your killer like He damned those who mutated into monkeys and boars.

Then, `Ábis ben Shabeeb Al-Shákiri came with Shawðab, the slave of Bani Shákir, and he said: O Shawðab what do you have in mind to do? He replied: what to do? I shall fight with you defending the son of the daughter of the prophet of Allah (PUH) until I get killed. He replied: this is my thought about you, so step before Abá `Abdilláh to recognize you like he did with the others, and to recognize you me myself for this is a day that we should ask for the rewards in by everything we can do, for there are no deeds after that, it is but the judgement after that. Then Shawðab stepped forward and said: peace upon you O Abá `Abdilláh and the may the mercy of Allah befall upon you and His blessings, I shall leave you with Allah. Then he fought until he got killed.

Then `Ábis stepped forward and said: O Abá `Abdilláh verily by Allah there is no one on the face of earth from far away or near by that can be more dear to myself than you, and if I could defend you against the unjust and being killed by something dearer than my soul and blood I would have done that, peace upon you O Abá `Abdilláh, and I make Allah a testifier for that I am on your path and the path of your father, then he went with his sword towards them directly and he had a mark on his forehead. Rabee` ben Tameem Al-Harithi said: when I saw him coming I knew him and I saw him many times in wars and he was one of the bravest people so I said (to the crowds): O people this is the lion of the lions the son of Shabeeb, the mighty, no one shall go out to combat with him, stone him, and so they did, and then `Ábis called: one man for one man, but the people avoided him for his bravery, and Ibn Sa`d [`Umar] then said: stone him severly, and they stoned him from all the sides, and when he saw that he dropped down his shield and his helmet and attacked the crowds and defeated them. The narrator said: by Allah, I saw him knocking out more than 200 from the crowds, and then they surrounded him from all sides and they killed him, then I saw his head at the hands of some men with their weapons, each of them say that he killed him, then Ibn Sa`d said: don't fight now, this man is not killed by one single man, so he resolved that issue among them.

Then Habeeb ben Mozháhir Al-Asdi showed up and said:

I am Habeeb and my father is Mozháhir
a knight of the wars and the fire that burns
Verily you are great in numbers
but we have the higher hands
And you betray at the time of loyalty
and we are more loyal than you and have the patience
Verily, we are more faithful than you all and better

Then, he fought bitterly and he killed a man from (the tribe of) Bani Tameem that was called Bodayl ben Soraym, and another man from Tameem attacked him and stabbed him, so he wanted to get up, then he received a strike from Al-Hosayn ben Tameem on his head with the sword and he fell down, and then the man of Tameem came down to him and beheaded him, and his death shocked Al-Husayn (PUH) and he said: by Allah I shall recognize myself and the protectors of my companions. Then Al-Hosayn said to the man of Tameem: I am your partner in killing him (Habeeb), the man replied: no by Allah (you're not). He said: give me the head to hang it on the neck of my horse to let the people see that I'm your partner in killing him and then take it back for I don't have any benefit from whatever Ibn Ziyád would give you. So, he gave him the head and he toured among the people with it and then returned it back to him and when he returned to Kufa he hanged it on the neck of his horse.

Then a turkish slave for Al-Husayn (PUH) that was called Aslam, and he was a Quran reader, he went out to fight while saying:

The sea is burning from my stabbing and hitting
and the air is full of my arrows and darts
When my sword is in my right hand raising up
The heart of the envious noble shall be torn in parts

Then he killed 70 men and fell down on the ground, and Al-Husayn (PUH) then came to him and cried and then put his cheek on his cheek, and then Aslam opened his eyes and saw Al-Husayn (PUH), then he smiled and his soul got out of his body.

Then, Borayr ben Khodhayr Al-Hamadáni got out and he was a faithful man and considered the best reader of Quran at his time and he was called "the master of readers" and he said:

I am Borayr and my father is Khodhayr
verily there is no blessings for him who has no goodness

Then he started to attack the crowds while saying: get closer to me you O killers of the believers, get closer to me O killers of the sons of those who were in Badr, get closer to me you O killers of the prophet's sons and his Household. Then, Yazeed ben Ma`qal got out for him and said: O Borayr how do you see what Allah has done with you? He replied: verily He made the goodness with me and the evil with you, then Yazeed said: you lied, and you were not a liar before this day, do you remember when I was walking with you among Bani Lawáðin and you were saying: `Uthmán was a squanderer over himself and Mo`áwiyah is astraying and made people astray, and the true leader of the guidance is `Ali ben Abi Tálib, then Borayr said: I testify that this is my saying and this is my opinion, and then Yazeed said: I testify that you are an astraying man. Then Borayr said: come on and let's pray humbly and invoke the curse of Allah over the liar (between us), and so they did and then they made a combat and struck each other two times, thus Yazeed hit Borayr lightly and did not harm him but Borayr struck him hardly on his helmet and made the sword go through until it reached his brain, so he fell down and the sword remained in his head. Then Radhi ben Monqið Al-`Abdi attacked Borayr and hugged him and fought for some time, and then Borayr threw him to the ground and sat on his chest, and Ka`b ben Jábir Al-Azdi stabbed him on his back with his spear, so Borayr got down from Ibn Monqið after biting his nose and cutting it, and then `Afeef ben Zohayr ben Abi Al-Akhnas shouted at him (at Ka`b): this is Borayr ben Khodhayr the reader, the one who was reading Quran to us in Kufa mosque, but he (Ka`b) didn't look at him and struck him with the sword until he killed him, may Allah be pleased with him.

And when Ka`b ben Jábir returned back from the battle later on, his wife said to him: you've helped against the son of Fatima and killed Borayr the master of the readersm verily I shall never talk to you again, and then he said:

[here comes a long poem describing how he is proud in fighting Al-Husayn]

And then, Wahab ben Habbáb Al-Kalbi raised and he was a christian, but turned into Islam by the hands of Al-Husayn (PUH) and he was with his mother and his wife, and his mother said: raise up O son and nourish the son of the daughter of the prophet of Allah (PUH), and he said: I shall do mother and not any less, so he raised up and said:

If you deny me then I am the son of Al-Kalbi
you shall see me and see my beating

And my attacks and fight in the war
after the revenge of my partners my revenge I shall be chasing
I shall push away the adversity in the face of the adversity
and my fighting in the war is verily not playing

Then he attacked until he killed some of them and got back to his wife and his mother, and he said: O mother, are you satisfied yet? She replied: I'm not satisfied unless you are killed defending Al-Husayn (PUH), and his wife said: by Allah, don't frighten me with yourself, and his mother said: O son, neglect her saying and get back to fight before the son of the daughter of your prophet, and you shall receive the intercession of his grandfather at the day of the judgement. He got back and fought until his both hands were amputated!! Then his wife took a pillar and ran towards him and said: may my father and my mother be ransoms for you, defend the kind people the Household of the prophet of Allah (PUH), and he said to her: you were advising me to stop fighting and now you're here to fight with me, and then she said: O Wahab, don't blame me, verily the cries of Al-Husayn have broken my heart. He asked: what did you hear him say? She said: O Wahab I saw him sitting at the enterance of the tent while he was crying and saying: Alas! No nourisher!! Then Wahab cried a lot and said to her: get back to the women may Allah have mercy upon you, but she denied and then Wahab shouted: my lord Abá `Abdilláh, let her get back to the tent, and so the imam did.

Then the people gathered around him and killed him, and his mother walked to him, and some say it was his wife, and sat down beside him rubbing the blood off his body and say: congratulations for you got the paradise, and I ask Allah who gave you the paradise to let me go with you.

Then Shimr said to his slave Rostom, hit her head, and so he did, and she died in her place and she was the first woman to die from the companions of Al-Husayn.

Then `Amr ben Qorzhah Al-Ansári raised up and took the permission from Al-Husayn and he allowed him to go, so he went and said:

Verily the phalanx of Al-Ansári knew
that I shall protect the boundaries of honor
Strikes of a kid that doesn't run away
and for Al-Husayn shall be my life and home

So then he fought like someone waiting for the reward until he killed so many of them, and no single arrow would arrive at Al-Husayn (PUH) that he wouldn't receive with his hand, or a sword that he wouldn't receive with his heart and so no harm reached Al-Husayn (PUH) until he was thickened with injuries and then he looked at Al-Husayn (PUH) and said: O son of the prophet of Allah, did I fullfil? He replied: yes, you are in front of me in paradise, so tell the prophet of Allah (PUH) my greetings and tell him that I will be there soon too. Then he fought until he got killed, may Allah be pleased with him. He had a brother who was with `Umar ben Sa`d who said to Al-Husayn (PUH): you've tricked my brother until you killed him? Then Al-Husayn (PUH) said to him: Allah did not trick your brother but verily He guided him and made you astray, and he said: may Allah kill me if I didn't kill you or I shall die, so he attacked but his way was blocked by Náfi` ben Hilál who stabbed him and got him down, and then companions saved him.

Then a young man whose father got killed in the battle raised up and his mother was with him, and she said to him: get out O son and fight before the son of the prophet of Allah (PUH), and then Al-Husayn (PUH) said: this is a young man whose father got killed in the battle maybe his mother hates to see him out there, then the young man said: my mother is the one who ordered me to go out! So he got out and said:

my prince is Husayn and what a prince is he
the gladness of the heart of the omen and warner
`Ali and Fatima are his parents
do you know anyone to him like similar
He has a face like the sun of the noon
and he has a beard like the bright moon

And then he fought until he got killed and got beheaded and his head was thrown towards the camp of Al-Husayn (PUH), so his mother then carried his head and said: good deed you've done my son, O the gladness of my heart and the gladness of my eyes. Then she threw the head of her son towards a man and she got him killed, and she took the pillar of the tent and attacked them while saying:

I am an old woman for my lord and weak
empty and thin I am and unable
I shall strike you bitterly
defending the sons of Fatima the honorable

And she struck two men and killed them, and Al-Husayn ordered to get her back and he prayed for her.

Then `Amr ben Khálid Al-Saydáwi raised up and said to Al-Husayn (PUH): O Abá `Abdilláh, verily I am now to follow my partners and I hated to leave and see you alone and dead, so Al-Husayn (PUH) said to him: advance, verily we shall follow you in some time. So he advanced and fought until he got killed.

Then, Hanzhalah ben As`ad Al-Shibámi came before Al-Husayn (PUH) to protect him against the arrows and the spears and the swords by his face and his neck. Then he called and said: O people, I am afraid for you a day like the day of the parties [day of parties a name of a battle that was between muslims and disbelievers], like the deeds of the people of Noah and `Ád and Thamood and those who came after them, and verily Allah doesn't wrong the bondmen. And, O people, I fear for you a Day of Summoning, when you run away and have nothing to protect you against Allah, O people don't kill Al-Husayn for verily Allah will destroy you by His punishment, and he shall be disappointed whoever spread the lies. Then Al-Husayn (PUH) said to him: O son of As`ad may Allah have mercy upon you, verily they deserved the punishment when they answered your calls previously and raised up to curse you with your companions, how is it now and they killed your faithful companions. He replied: you are right, may I be a ransom for you, shouldn't we go to our Lord and follow our brothers? He (Al-Husayn) said: for sure, go to something better from this life and what is in it and to an eternal fortune. He then said: peace upon you O son of the prophet of Allah (PUH) and upon your Household and may we be together in heaven, and then Al-Husayn replied: Amen, Amen. So he went out to the crowds and fought bitterly until he got killed.

Then Náfi` ben Hilál Al-Jamli raised up and fought fiercely and he was shooting the crowds with poisoned arrows and his name was written on them and he was saying:

I shall throw it and their tops are marked
and the soul shall see no benefit from its fearing
Poisoned that goes within its heart
to fill the land from its spreading

And he kept on shooting at them until he had no more, and then he held his sword and took it out and said:

I am the kid of Al-Jamali from Yemen
verily the creed of Husayn and `Ali is my creed
If I got killed this day, this is my hope
and this is what I see and shall meet my deed

So they broke his two arms and he was taken a prisoner, and Shimr took him to Ibn Sa`d, and Ibn Sa`d said to him: woe to you! O Náfi` what made you do that with yourself? He replied: my Lord knows better what I wanted, and the blood was going down on his beard and his face and then he said: I've killed 12 men from you adding to that those I've injured and if I had an arm left you wouldn't be able to capture me, then Shimr took his sword out to kill him and Náfi` said to him: by Allah if you were a muslim it would be so horriblefor you to meet Allah with our blood, so praise be to Allah that He made our deaths by the most devilish creatures of His creations, and then Shimr killed him.

Then, Jawn [not John] the slave of Abá Ðar Al-Ghifári raised up and he was a black slave, and Al-Husayn (PUH) said to him: you have my permission to stay away, you've followed us for goodness so don't be troubled in our own way, so he said: O son of the prophet of Allah (PUH) I lick your dishes in the good times, and in adversity I shall let you down? Then by Allah my smell shall be disgusting! and my ancestry shall be the most devilish! And verily my color shall be black! So, breath on me from the paradise, thus my smell would be the nicest and my ancestry shall be the best! And my face shall be the whitest! No by Allah, I shall never leave you until this black blood get mixed with your own bloods, and then he raised up and said:

How do the disbelievers see the beats of the black
by the sword I beat defending the Household of Mohammed
I shall protect them by the tongue and by the hand
and seek the paradise later at the day of judgement

Then he battled until he got killed, and then Al-Husayn (PUH) stood up and said: Allahoma, make his face white! And turn his smell into good! and make him with the faithful, and make him meet the Household of Mohammed (PUH).

Then one man after the other from the companions of Al-Husayn (PUH) used to come to Al-Husayn (PUH) and say: peace upon you O son of the prophet of Allah, and Al-Husayn (PUH) would say: and peace upon you and we shall be behind you, and then say: Some of them have paid their vow by death (in battle), and some of them still are waiting. So, until all of them were killed and only Al-Husayn was left with his family only and they are the children of `Ali (PUH) and the sons of Ja`far (PUH) [the brother of imam `Ali], and the sons of `Aqeel (PUH) [the brother of imam `Ali], and the sons of imam Al-Hasan (PUH) [the brother of imam Al-Husayn], and the sons of Al-Husayn (PUH), so they gathered together to pay farewell for each other, and decided to fight, and they were 17 men and some say there were more.

Then `Ali ben Al-Husayn Al-Akbar (PUH) raised up, and his mother was Laylá bent Abi-Morrah ben `Urwah ben Mas`ood, and her mother was Maymoonah bent Abi Sufyán ben Harb, and he was one with a bright face and people never see like him, and had the nicest manners and his age was 18 and some say it was 25, and he was married and was a target for poets, and some said about him

The eye never saw someone like him
who walks with bare foot and with sandals
I mean the son of Laylá the noble

I mean the son of the daughter of the great lineages
This life is nothing for his faithfulness
and never give the truth in change of the false

Then he asked for his father's permission to fight, and he gave him the permission and then looked at him a look of someone despaired of him, and then he closed his eyes and cried, and then raised his index finger to the sky and said: Allahoma, testify over them that they are fighting a young man who is the most like of the prophet in shape and manners and in speech, and whenever we liked to see Your prophet we would look at him. Allahoma, forbid them the blesses of the earth and separate them into bands and tear them severely, and make them torn into groups and never make the viceroys satisfied with them, for they called us to nourish us and then they've been aggressive towards us to fight us.

Then he shouted: O Ibn Sa`d, may Allah cut off your lineage and may He never bless you in your matters and may He appoint someone to kill you after me while you're on your bed, like the way you cut off my lineage and did not save my closeness from the prophet of Allah (PUH).

Then he raised his voice and said: Lo! Allah preferred Adam and Noah and the Family of Abraham and the Family of 'Imran above (all His) creatures. They were descendants one of another. Allah is Hearer, Knower.

Then `Ali attacked the crowds and he was saying:

I am `Ali ben Al-Husayn ben `Ali
we and the House of Allah are better for the prophet
by Allah the son of the bastard shall not rule us

and I shall strike with the sword defending my father
like the strikes of a hashimite, an `Alawite

Then he attacked them and then returned back to his father and said: O father, the thirst killed me and the heaviness of the iron made me exhausted, any way for a sip of water? Then Al-Husayn (PUH) cried and said: Alas! any help! O son, from where should I get the water? Fight a little for you will see your grandfather Mohammed (PUH) in a while, and he shall make you drink from his abundant cup such a drink that you will never become thirsty at all. Then he started to fight one time after the other and the kufans were avoiding killing him, and then Morrah ben Monqið Al-`Abdi looked him and said: may the burdens of Arabs be over my back if he did what he is doing and passed me by and I wouldn't bereave his mother! Then he passed by attacking the crowds like he used to do and Morrah ben Monqið blocked his way and hit him and some say he stabbed him with a spear and killed him, and then he called: O father peace upon you, this is my grandfather saying peace upon you and asking you to come in a hurry (to us), and then the people surrounded him and cut him with their swords, and then Al-Husayn (PUH) came until he stood over his body and said: may Allah kill the people who killed you O son, how dare are they against the Merciful and for attacking the Household of the prophet; verily life after you is nothing. Then Zaynab bent `Ali (PUH) [the sister of Al-Husayn] went out calling: Alas! my beloved! Alas! the son of my brother! She came and dropped herself down over him, and Al-Husayn (PUH) came to her and took her hand and turned her back to the tent, and then called his sons and asked them to carry their brother from his place of death, until they put him in front of the tent that they were fighting in front of it.

Then, `Abdullah ben Muslim ben `Aqeel ben Abi Tálib, and his mother was Roqayyah bent `Ali ben Abi Tálib, he raised up and said:

Today I shall meet Muslim and he is my father
and some men that were killed before the prophet's religion
They are not some people that were some liars
but the best of people and the best of lineage
from Háshim the masters and people of the ancestry

So he killed some people in 3 campaigns, and then Zayd ben Warqá' shot an arrow at him and he received with his hand, and it got hanged to his forehead and he couldn't remove it from his forehead, and then he said: Allahoma, they let us down and humiliated us, so kill them like they killed us, and then he shot another arrow at him, and another man stabbed him with his spear in the heart, and so he died peace upon him.

Then Mohammed ben Muslim ben `Aqeel (PUH) raised up and fought until he got killed. He was killed by Abu-Jorhom Al-Azdi and Laqeet ben Yásir Al-Johani.

Then Mohammed ben Abi-Sa`eed ben `Aqeel (PUH) raised and fought until he got killed. He was killed by Laqeet ben Yásir Al-Johani by an arrow.

Then Ja`far ben `Aqeel (PUH) raised while saying:

I am the man from Tálib
from people of Háshim and Ghálib
We are truely the masters of honor
and this is Al-Husayn the best of the best
From the Household of the faithful and the victorious

So he killed 15 knights and two men, and then he got killed by `Abdulláh ben `Urwah Al-Khath`imi.

Then `Abdul-Rahmán ben `Aqeel (PUH) raised while saying:

My father is `Aqeel so know my place
in Háshim and Háshim are my brothers
Old men of truth and the masters of their likes
This is Al-Husayn like the greatest structures
And the master of the old men with the youth

So he killed 17 knights, and then `Uthmán ben Khálid Al-Johani with Bishr ben Sawt attacked him and killed him.

Then `Abdullah Al-Akbar ben `Aqeel (PUH) raised up and fought fiercely and then got killed by `Uthmán ben Khálid Al-Johani with Bishr ben Sawt.

Then Mohammed ben `Abdulláh ben Ja`far ben Abi Tálib (PUH) and his mother was Al-Khawsá' who was from the tribe of Tayyim Al-Lát ben Tha`labah, he raised up and said:

Verily I complain to Allah from the aggression
(I am) the killer of people that are blind in the war
They departed the meanings of the Quran
and the revealed laws and teachings
And showed the disbelieving and the agression

Then he fought until he killed 10 of them, then he was attacked by `Ámir ben Nahshal Al-Tamimi and got killed.

Then his brother `Awn ben `Abdulláh ben Ja`far (PUH) and his mother was Zaynab the daughter of the prince of the believers (PUH) raised up and said:

If you deny me verily I am the son of Ja`far

the martyr of the truth and in paradise he blossoms
He shall fly in it with a green wing
this is enough for pride at the day of judgement

Then he fought until he killed 3 knights and 18 men, and then was attacked by `Abdulláh ben Qotbah and got killed.

Then Al-Qásim ben Al-Hasan ben `Ali ben Abi Tálib (PUT) raised up, and he was a young kid, and when Al-Husayn (PUH) saw him raising up to fight, he hugged him and both of them cried until then fell into coma. Then he asked his uncle for a permission to fight, but he denied to do so, and the kid kept kissing his hands and his feet until he decided to give a permission for him, so he went out and his tears upon his cheeks and said:

If you deny me then I am the son of Al-Hasan
the grandson of the prophet the chosen and the entrusted
This is Husayn like the prisoner who kept as a hostage
among people that shall not be watered by the clouds

And he fought bitterly, and he killed despite his young age 35 men. Hameed ben Muslim said: a kid went out towards us and his face was like the moon, and there was a sword in his hand, and wearing a shirt and a cloth on his loin and sandals in his feet, and the tie of one of his sandals was cut and I don't forget that it was the left, and then `Amr ben Sa`d ben Nofayl Al-Azdi said to me: the burdens of Arabs shall be on my back if I didn't bereave his uncle Al-Husayn when he passes me by doing this, and I said: sanctified is Allah, and what do you want by that? by Allah if he beat me I shall not raise my hand towards him! Leave him alone, those who surround him are enough, and he replied: by Allah I shall attack him. Then he attacked him and hit his head with the sword and killed him, and the kid fell down to the ground on over his face and shouted: O uncle! And Al-Husayn

(PUH) showed up like the hawk and attacked like the angry lion and hit `Amr ben Sa`d ben Nofayl with the sword and he received it with his elbow and it was amputated and screamed out loud that all the camp heard him, and Al-Husayn (PUH) turned away from him and the kufans came to rescue him but the horses stepped over `Amr with their hooves until he died, and the dust cleared out and there was Al-Husayn (PUH) standing over the head of the kid while he was striking with his legs while Al-Husayn (PUH) was saying: Far be they those people who killed you, and those whose their opponent about you is your grandfather and your father. Then he (PUH) said: it is hard for your uncle not to call him and he wouldn't respond or respond and no voice would help you, by Allah there are many of his killers and so few are his nourishers. Then he took him and put his chest over his chest and like I can see the legs of the kid touching the ground, and he took him until he put him down with his son `Ali Al-Akbar and the rest of the dead from his own family. Then he said: Allahoma make them few in numbers and kill them to their last and never leave single on of them, and when I asked about the kid they told me: this is Al-Qásim ben Al-Hasan ben `Ali ben Abi Tálib (PUH).

Then Al-Husayn (PUH) shouted in that situation: O patience children of my brothers, O patience O people of my Household, by Allah you shall not see a humiliating day ever after this day.

Then Abu-Bakr ben Al-Hasan ben `Ali ben Abi Tálib (PUH) raised up and fought until he got killed. He was shot by an arrow by `Abdulláh ben `Uqbah Al-Ghanawi and some say Harmalah ben Káhil.

Then the brothers of Al-Husayn (PUH) raised up desiring to die before him! The first to raise was: Abu-Bakr ben `Ali ben Abi Tálib and his name was `Ubaydilláh and his mother was Laylá bent Mas`ood, from the tribe of Nahshal. So he advanced while saying:

My sheik is `Ali of the longest proud lineage
from Háshim he is, of the truth and the grace
This is Husayn the son of the prophet who was sent
and we shall protect him with the sharp swords
My life shall be ransom for him O what a brother of mine

Then he fought until he got killed by Zajr ben Badr Al-Nakh`ee. Then his brother `Umar ben `Ali (PUH) raised after him while saying:

I shall beat you without any mercy
that bastard verily he disbelieved the prophet
O Zijr O Zijr come closer to `Umar
verily you'll meet today the hell of Saqar
[Saqar is one of the names of hell]

Then he attacked Zijr the killer of his brother and he killed him. Then he received the crowds and started to beat them with his sword bitterly while saying:

Go away O enemies of Allah go away from `Umar
go away from the lion that crushes and frawns
Shall strike you with the sword and never run away
and not in war like the coward that returns

So he kept fighting until he got killed, may the peace of Allah be upon him.

Then Mohammed Al-Asghar ben `Ali ben Abi Tálib (PUH) raised up, and he was shot by an arrow by a man from Tameem, from the children of Abán ben Dárim, so he killed him and brought his head.

Then `Abdulláh ben `Ali (PUH) raised up and his mother was Laylá bent Mas`ood from Nahshal, and he fought until he got killed.

Then when Al-`Abbás ben `Ali (PUH) saw the large number of deads among his family he said to his brothers by his father and mother and they are: `Abdulláh and Ja`far and `Uthmán and their mother was Um-Albaneen bent Khálid ben Hozám from the tribe of Kiláb, and her original name was Fatima, he said to them: O children of my mother, advance so I can see you in good for the sake of Allah and His prophet.

Then `Abdulláh ben `Ali (PUH) raised and he was 25 years old and was saying:

I am the son of him of the help and the virtues
that is `Ali the good, the one of the deeds
The sword of the prophet of Allah that is fierce
every day verily is showing his fierce deeds

Then he fought with Háni ben Thobayt Al-Hadhrami and he got killed by Háni.

Then after him his brother Ja`far ben `Ali (PUH) raised up while saying:

I am Ja`far one of the high places
the son of `Ali the good man of the deeds
My ancestry by my uncle and my (motherly) uncle is the proudest

Then he was attacked by Háni ben Thobayt Al-Hadhrami as well and he killed him and brought his head, and some say he was shot by Khiwallá on his head or in his eye.

Then his brother `Uthmán ben `Ali raised up and took the place of his brothers and he was 21 years old and he was saying:

Verily I am `Uthmán the one of the pride
my sheik is `Ali the one of the purified deeds
This is Husayn the kindest of the kindest
and the master of the great men and the humbles
After the prophet he is the viceroy and the nourisher

Then Khiwallá ben Yazeed Al-Asbahi shot an arrow at his forehead and he fell down from his horse and then a man from the tribe of Abán ben Dárim came and killed him and beheaded him.

Then after them, their brother Al-`Abbás (PUH) raised up and he was the eldest and as 34 years old and his title was Abul-Fadhl, and was called also "The Water Bringer" and "The Moon of The Hashimites" and he was the owner of the banner of Al-Husayn (PUH), and he was handsome and pretty with a huge body, if he rode the horse, his legs would touch he ground, and he was the last one to stay with Al-Husayn, so he asked for a permission from his brother A-Husayn (PUH) to fight, and Al-Husayn (PUH) said to him: O my brother, you are owner of my banner, and Al-`Abbas (PUH) said: my chest is getting narrow and I want to take the revenge from those hypocrites, and then Al-Husayn (PUH) said: then, go and bring some water for these children. Then Al-`Abbás when to the crowds and warned them against the wrath of the Almighty but that was not useful! Then he got back to Al-Husayn (PUH) to tell him what happened, but he heard the children shout: the thirst! the thirst! So he took his horse and took the skin (for water) and reached Al-Forát, and then he was surrounded by 4 thousands and they started shooting arrows at him but he didn't care about their gatherings and was not afraid of their numbers and he said:

I am the who is known by the fierce shout
known as the son of `Ali, who is called Haydarah

And he turned them away from the banks and then he got into the water and took a sip in his hand to drink, but he remembered the thirst of Al-Husayn (PUH), so he dropped the water from his hand and said:

O my soul be lowered down after Al-Husayn
and after him you shall not ever be
This is Al-Husayn the drinker of the death
and you want to drink the cold water?
by Allah this is not the deeds of my creed
and not the deeds of a man of true belief

Then he filled the skin with water and headed to the camp and they blocked his way, so he started to beat them and say:

I am not afraid of death if death shows up
until I get buried by the sharpened swords
I am Al-`Abbás and I shall go with the water
and I am not afraid of the evil at battles
And my soul shall be a shield for the purified grandson of the prophet

Then he turned them away from his way, and Zayd ben Warqá' Al-Johani hided behind a palm tree, and struck him on his right hand and amputated it, so he took the sword with his left hand and attacked while saying:

By Allah if you cut my right
verily I shall protect my creed forever
And defend an imam truthful in belief
the son of the prophet, the purified and the entrusted

Then Hakeem ben Tofayl hided behind a palm tree, and struck him on his left and amputated it, so he hugged the banner to his chest and said:

O my soul don't be afraid of the disbelievers
and be glad with the mercy of the Almighty
With the prophet, the chosen master
by their sinful manners they cut off my left
So my Lord make them feel the fire of hell

Then they gathered around him and the arrows arrived at him like the rain, and one arrow struck the skin and the water poured down, and another one struck his chest and another one struck his eye, and then a man struck him with a pillar on his head and he fell down to the ground while calling: peace upon you from me O Abá `Abdilláh, and some say that he said: peace upon you from me O Abá `Abdillah, help me O brother.

And then Al-Husayn (PUH) came to him and saw his both hands amputated and thickened with injuries, and then he bent over him and cried out loud and said: now verily my backbone had been broken and my tricks are not much to be done.

Then he attacked the enemies and struck them right and left and all of them escaped before him like the goat that escapes from the wolf, while he was saying: to where are you escaping and you killed my brother? where to you escape and you've killed my helper, until he turned the enemies away from Abul-Fadhl, and while Al-Husayn (PUH) was sitting beside his brother

Al-`Abbás, his (Al-`Abbás') soul got released and Al-Husayn left him at that place.

Then Al-Husayn stood up and went back to the camp with a broken back and sadness and crying, and cleaning his tears from his eyes with his sleeves, and then Sokaynah [his daughter] came to him and asked about her uncle (Al-`Abbás), and he told her that he got killed, and Zaynab heard him saying that so she shouted: Alas! my brother! Alas! `Abbás! Alas! how are we lost after you! And the women cried and Al-Husayn cried with them and said: Alas! how are we lost after you! And when Al-`Abbás got killed, Al-Husayn looked around and so no one that would nourish him, and he looked at his family and his companions and they were all butchered like the sheeps, while he was hearing the women and children cry out loud, and then he called out loud: any one that would nourish the Household of the prophet (PUH)? Any believer that would fear Allah for us? Any helper that likes to meet Allah by helping us? Any helper that likes what Allah has for him for helping us? And the voices of the women raised with crying.

Then he went to the enterance of the tent and said to Zaynab: give me my infant to pay him the farewell, and they brought him his son `Abdulláh, and his mother was Al-Rabáb bent Imri' Al-Qays Al-Kalbi, so he took him and put him in his lap and bent over him to kiss him, but Harmalah ben Káhil Al-Asdi shot him with an arrow that got into his neck and killed him, and then he said to Zaynab: take him, and he took the blood with his hand and when it was full he threw the blood towards the sky [and some say no drop came down to earth] and said: (O Allah) make it easy for me what happened with him verily it is under the eyes of Allah, Allahoma don't let him be lower in value than Faseel [the breed of the camel of the prophet Sálih. Check the prophets in islamic literature]. Then he carried him and put him with the dead people of his Household, and some say that he dug a grave for him by the edge of his sword and buried him there.

Then Al-Husayn (PUH) advanced toward the crowds and raising his sword and despaired of life and called the people for a combat, and he killed everyone that met him, until he killed so many of them. Then he attacked the right wing and said:

To be killed is better than being ashamed
and the shame is better than going to hell
by Allah this and that are not my companions

Then he attacked the left wing and said:

I am Al-Husayn ben `Ali
I've sworn not to bend
I shall protect the children of my father
and go on with the way of the prophet

some narrators said: by Allah, we've never seen a bereaved man that lost all his children and his Household and his companion in his likes of bravery, by Allah I've never seen one like him before or after him, and when the men gather around him to attack he would strike them with his sword and make them tear away from his right and left like the goat that is attacked by the wolf! He was attacking them and their numbers completed the 30 thousands and all of them are defeated before like the locusts and then he would return to the center and say: verily there is no power except by Allah.

When Shimr saw that, he ordered the knights to be at the back of the foot soldiers and then ordered the archers to shoot at him and so they did until his shield became like a hedgehog, and then Shimr came with some fellows and blocked the way between him and his harem! Then Al-Husayn (PUH) shouted: woe to you! O followers of Abu-Sufyán, if you have no religion and were not afraid of the judgement day then be free in this life and turn back to your ancestries if you were Arabs as you claim, then Shimr called him and said: what are you saying O son of Fatima? Then he replied: I say, I am fighting you and you are fighting me and the women have no guilt, so turn away your ignorant people and your tyrants and don't let them attack my harem as long I am alive. Then Shimr said: you've got that O son of Fatima, and then he shouted: stay away from the harem of the man and point at him directly, by my life he is a graceful man! So they pointed at him for fighting and Shimr was stirring up the people to fight Al-Husayn (PUH), and they attacked him and he would attack them back and they turn away from his way, and he was asking for a drop of water but couldn't find any.

Then he attacked in the direction of Al-Forát, against `Amr ben Al-Hajjáj with 4 thousands men, and he exposed them away from the water, and got into the water with the horse, and when the horse started to drink, Al-Husayn (PUH) said: you are thirsty and I am thirsty and I shall not drink until you drink, and horse raised his head up like if he understood the talk! Then when Al-Husayn (PUH) extended his arm to drink the water, a man called him and said: do you drink the water while your harem is exposed? Then he dropped the water and didn't drink and heading to the tent (to protect his harem), and then he (PUH) got back to fight the enemies of Allah and remained in the fight until he was injured with 72 injuries. Then he stood to take a rest and he was weak to continue fighting, and while he was standing, Abul-Hotoof Al-Jo`fi threw a stone to him, and some say with an arrow, and it hit his forehead, so he took a cloth to clean the blood from his forehead, and while doing so a poisoned arrow with three heads arrived into his heart! Then he (PUH) said: by the name of Allah and by Allah, and on the way of the prophet of Allah, then he raised his head to the sky and said: O my Lord, verily You know that they are killing a man that has no likings on earth, and then he took the arrow and got him out from his back and the blood gushed out like the rain! The blood gushing made him exhausted so he sat on the ground and turning his neck around, and in that situation, Málik ben Al-Nisr Al-Kindi came to him and cursed him and hit his honorable head with the sword, and there was a cloak over his head, and the cloak got filled with blood, and Al-Husayn (PUH): may you never eat with your hand neither drink, and may Allah gather you with the wrong people, and then he threw the cloak away and put his hood.

And in that situation, `Abdulláh ben Al-Hasan (PUH) got out and he was a lad of 11 years, and he went to his uncle Al-Husayn, and Zaynab then went after him to keep him away, and Al-Husayn (PUH) said to her: O my sister keep him away, but the lad denied fiercely and came to his uncle Al-Husayn (PUH) and stood beside him and said: I shall not leave my uncle, then Bahr ben Ka`b wanted to wind his sword to Al-Husayn (PUH) and the lad said to him: woe to you! O son of the bad woman! you want to kill my uncle! Then Bahr ben Ka`b struck him with the sword and he received it with his hand and it was amputated to the skin and remained hanged up, and the kid called: Alas! my uncle! or Alas! O my mother! And then Al-Husayn (PUH) took him and hugged him to his chest and said: O son of my brother be patient for the adversities that befell upon you and wait for the goodness, for verily Allah will make you follow your good fathers and the prophet of Allah (PUH) and `Ali (PUH) and Hamzah and Ja`far and Al-Hasan (PUT), and then Harmalah ben Káhil threw at him an arrow and killed him in the lap of his uncle, and then Al-Husayn (PUH) raised his hand and said: Allahoma forbid them the rains of the skies and forbid them the blessings of the earth, Allahoma if you made them live for a while then let them be separated severely and make them tear apart in bands, and never make their rulers be satisfied with them, for they have invited us to support us and then attacked us to kill us.

Then Al-Husayn (PUH) remained on the ground for some time although they could have killed him, but every tribe was depending on the other and hated to do so.

Hilál ben Náfi` said: I was standing with the fellows of `Umar ben Sa`d when a caller shouted: O be happy prince, this is Shimr killed Al-Husayn, so I went out between the two rows and took a look at him and I've seen him protecting himself, and by Allah, I've never seen a man that got dipped in his blood that would be better than him, and no one with a face brighter than his, and I was busy looking at the halo of his face and the beauty of his shape and didn't think of killing him, and while he was in that situation he asked for water, and I heard a man saying: by Allah you shall not drink the water until you go to hell and drink from its fire, and I heard him reply: I shall go to hell and drink of its fire? No by Allah, I shall go to my grandfather the prophet of Allah (PUH) and shall live with him in his own home in a firmly established in the favour of a Mighty King, and I shall drink a water that is not dirty and I shall complain to him about you've done to me, and all of them got angry like if Allah never planted anything of mercy in their hearts.

Then Al-Husayn (PUH) raised his hand to the sky and said: Allahoma, O You of the High Place, of the Mighty Power, of the Great Wisdom, not in need of the creatures, and high in His Pride, verily You are Able for whatever You desire, close in mercy, and true with the promise, and Graceful with His favors, and a Tester of goodness, close whenever You are called, and surrounding whatever You have created, and verily You accept the repenting for those who repent, and verily You are Able for what You desire, and verily You get whatever You want, Thankful if You have been praised, and You mention those who mention You, and I pray to You for my need, and ask You for my necessity, and go toward You when I am afraid and cry for my adversities, and I seek help from You when I am weak, and I depend on You when I am satisfied, Allahoma, judge between us and between those people for they have tricked us and let us down and betrayed us and killed us, and we are the Household of Your prophet, and the children of Your beloved Mohammed (PUH), the one who You have chosen him for the Message, and made him to receive the inspirations, so make for us, O Lord, a relief from our matter O You the most Merciful of all. Patience over what You have destined O Lord, no other god but You, O Helper of those who need the help.

Then Shimr shouted at the knights and the foot soldiers: woe to you! what do you wait from the man? Kill him may your mothers be bereaved, and so they attacked him from all the sides and Zor`ah ben Shorayk hit him on his left shoulder, and Al-Husayn (PUH) hit Zor`ah and killed him. Then another man hit him on his holy shoulder with his sword and made him fall on his face, and he was sitting. Then he started to stand up and fall down, and then Sinán ben Anas Al-Nakh`ee stabbed him in his throat and took the spear out and stabbed him in his chest, and threw him with an arrow into his neck, so he then fell down and sat on the ground and took the arrow out from his neck and started to collect the blood with his hands and whenever they were full he would paint his head and his beard with it while saying: this is how shall I meet Allah, painted with blood and my rights have been taken.

Then `Umar ben Sa`d said to Sinán ben Anas: get down woe to you! go to Al-Husayn (PUH) and make him rest, and then Sinán said to Khiwallá ben Yazeed: go and behead him, and Khiwallá went to do so but he got weakened and shocked, so Sinán said to him and some say Shimr said to him: may Allah disolve you arms, why are you shaking? Then Sinán got down and some say it was Shimr and he killed him and amputated his holy head while saying: I behead you and I know you are the master and the son of the prophet of Allah and the best of people from mother's and father's side, and then he gave the head to Khiwallá and said to him: take it to the prince `Umar ben Sa`d.

Then the crowds came to steal whatever he (PUH) had, thus his shirt was taken by Is-háq ben Khawiyyah Al-Hadhrami, and his pants were taken by Bahr ben Ka`b and his turban was taken by Al-Akhnas, and his shield was taken by `Umar ben Sa`d, and his clothes were taken by a brother of Is-háq ben Khawiyyah, and his velvet was taken by Qays ben Al-Ash`ath ben Qays, and his cloak was taken by Málik ben Nisr, and his sword was taken by Al-Faláfis Al-Nahshali from the tribe of Dárim, and his sandals were taken by Al-Aswad ben Khálid, and his ring was taken by Bajdal ben Saleem Al-Kalbi who amputated the finger with the ring.

THE SECOND PART

Introduction

THE history kept reviving the rememberance of 40 days passing the martyrdom of the eternal hero and the first revolutionist in Islam: Al-Husayn ben `Ali ben Abi Tálib (PUT), and the rememberance of the turn back of the prisoners of the Household of the prophet and Al-Husayn (PUT) to Karbala, to set the fineral ceremony over the tomb of Abá `Abdilláh, Al-Husayn (PUH).

In this day, in every year since 14 centuries, Karbala is wearing the clothes of moruning and get condensed with the crowds and visitors that came from all around the islamic world to fill the streets and the roads and the compleces in thousands, for the commemoration of "the fourtieth" [C] of Al-Husayn (PUH) [In eastern cultures, specifically islamic ones, the mourning of women with their black clothes remain for 40 days after the death of their man, and it is called mainly Al-Arba`een, literally: The Fourtieth, which means the pass of 40 days].

Thus, all of Karbala becomes a great place of commemoration that contains different persons from different islamic identities, so much that you cannot even pass through the large numbers of crowds and your eyes won't fall upon anything except of the heads of the crowds with signs of sadness upon their faces, and only hear the voice of the mourner and he is telling the story of the martyrdom of Al-Husayn (PUH) and the adversities of imprisoning the women and children of the Household of the prophet (PUH), and what happened to them in their journey from Karbala to Kufa, and from Kufa to Shám (Damascus), and how the fear of the situation and the fear from the enemies and the hard adversities that befell them never kept them away from doing their duties towards the revolution of Al-Husayn (PUH), and to spread the noble goals and explain them by those speeches in Kufa and in front of `Ubaydilláh ben Ziyád [the viceroy of Kufa for the Umayyads], and in the markets of Damascus and in the court of Yazeed ben Mo`áwiyah, which include as well the speeches of Zaynab Al-Kubra [or Zaynab the Great, Zynab bent `Ali (PUH), the sister of Al-Husayn] and Um-Kalthoom [another sister of Al-Husayn] and `Ali ben Al-Husayn (PUH) [the 4th imam] in the Umayyad Mosque [Arabic: Al-Jámi` Al-Umawi].

Yes, that speech that was out loud and shaked the throne of Yazeed and awakened the nations that went under the humiliation.

Here is it, the second part of the epical story of the martyrdom of Al-Husayn (PUH), which its first part was broadcasted on the day of Ashurah, which is kindly narrated here by the preacher of Karbala, the pilgrim, sheik `Abdul-Zahrá' Al-Ka`bee for this occasion:

[a long poem comes here first]

Al-Sayid Ibn Tawoos [a historian's name] say: then the crowds raced through to plunder the houses (tents) of the Household of the prophet and (the Household of) Fatima, so then the daughters of the prophet of Allah and the harem went out crying to each other and mourn for the protectors and the beloved ones.

Hameed ben Muslim said: and I saw a woman from the tribe of Bakr ben Wá'il who was with her husband among the fellows of

'Umar ben Sa`d, and when she saw the crowds breaking into the tents and plundering the women of Al-Husayn, she took a sword and headed to the tents and said: O you tribe of Bakr ben Wá'il! Are the daughters of the prophet being plundered!? No judge save but Allah!! Alas! The revenge of the prophet of Allah. Then her husband took her back to the camp.

Then they banished the women from the tents and set the fire in them (the tents), and they (the women) went out unveiled and plundered, and bare-footed and crying out loud, and they said to the enemies: by the rights of Allah, show us the place of Al-Husayn, and so they did and when the women looked at the dead people, they shouted out loud and slapped their faces. [a poem].

The narrator says: by Allah, I shall never forget Zaynab bent `Ali while she was mourning Al-Husayn and calling with a sad voice and a broken sad heart: Alas! Mohammed! The angels of heaven prayed upon you. This is Al-Husayn covered with his blood, and his parts are amputated, and his turban and cloak are plundered and your daughters are hostages. To Allah shall be the complaint and to Mohammed the Chosen, and to `Ali Al-Mortadhá and to Fatima Al-Zahrá' and to Hamzah the lord of the martyrs. Alas! Mohammed! This is Husayn in the desert, with his head been cut from the back. [a short poem].

Then, Sokayna bent Al-Husayn asked her aunt (Zaynab): to whom you are speaking? She answered her: your father Al-Husayn, and then she dropped down from her place to the body of her father ad hugged his corpse, and made all the enemies cry, and then `Umar ben Sa`d said: take her away from the body of her father, and then a group of nomads came and pulled her away from the body of her father, and she went away with her tears falling down.

The narrator said: then, `Umar ben Sa`d sent the head of Al-Husayn (PUH) at the day of Ashurah with Khiwallá ben Yazeed Al-Asbahi and Hameed ben Muslim to `Ubaydillah ben Ziyád, and ordered to bring the heads of the other companions and the Household (of Al-Husayn), so they were all amputated and he did it with Shimr ben Ðil-Jawshan and Qays ben Al-Ash`ath and `Amr ben Al-Hajjáj, and they went to Kufa, and `Umar ben Sa`d toured with whoever was left from the children of Al-Husayn and carried his (Al-Husayn's) women on the backs of the camels and they are the trusts of the prophets, and toured them like the hostages of turks and romans (byzantines), with lot of adversities and sadness.

It is narrated that the heads of the companions of Al-Husayn were 78 heads, and they were divided among the tribes so that may they make advances to Ibn Ziyád and to Yazeed.

So, the tribe of Kindah came up with 13 heads and their leader was Qays ben Al-Ash`ath, and the tribe of Hawázin came up with 12 heads and their leader was Shimr ben Ðil-Jawshan. And the tribe of Tameem came up with 17 heads, and the tribe of Asad came up with 16 heads, and the tribe of Moðhaj came up with 7 heads, and the rest of the heads were taken by the the people.

Then when Ibn Sa`d left Karbala, some people from the tribe of Asad came out and prayed upon these purified corpses and buried them as is it now.

Then, Ibn Sa`d toured with the afore mentioned hostages and when he reached Kufa, the people gathered to take a look at them, and one woman of the kufans came out and asked: what prisoners are you? And the daughters of `Ali replied: we are the prisoners from the Household of Mohammed, so she came down from the roof of her house and gathered some clothes and veils for them and gave them.

The roads got stuck in front of the Household by the people and the people of Kufa started to mourn and cry.

Then `Ali ben Al-Husayn (PUH) said: you mourn and cry for us? Then who killed us?

Basheer ben Khozaym Al-Asadi said: then I took a look at Zaynab bent `Ali (PUH) at that day, and I've never seen a shy woman who has an eloquent speech like her, like if she was talking by the tongue of her father, the prince of the believers, `Ali ben Abi Tálib (PUH), and she made a sign with her hand and all the people got silent. So then the breathes were taken and the bells went silent, and then she said: praising shall be to Allah, and blessings shall be on my father, Mohammed and his purified and kind Household. And then, O people of Kufa, O people of treachery and tricks! Do you cry? The tear shall not be dry and the weeping shall never stop, but the likes of you is like unto her who unravelleth the thread, after she hath made it strong, to thin filaments, making your oaths a deceit between you. Verily, is there anyone among you but the swaggerer and the rude? And the angry and the behated? And the adulation of maids and the trickery of the enemies, or like a pasture on the remains, or like a silver on a grave. Verily, evil is what your souls have given to yourselves to compile the wrath of Allah upon you, and in the Punishment you shall remain eternal. Do you cry? Do you weep? yes by Allah, cry a lot and laugh a little, for you've done its (the life) shame and disgrace, and you shall never wash it away, and how shall you make yourselves clear from killing the descendant of the prophet, and the core of the Message, and the lord of the youth in paradise? The one you are (supposed to) turn to in your troubles and adversities, and your cause and the applier of your creed? Verily, evil is what you've done, and far you may be and destroyed! Verily your efforts were disappointed, and your hands were cut down, and your deal is a losing one, and you've received the wrath of Allah, and humiliation shall be forced upon you. Woe to you O people of Kufa, do you know what a liver for the prophet you have fought against? And what blood for him you have shed? And what dignified daughter of him you have exposed? And what sanctity you have violated? You've came to it (life) with its baldness and stupidity and mis-shaped, like the dust of the ground and the air of the sky. Are you amazed for the sky to be raining blood upon you? Verily the punishment of the judgement day is even worse and more shameful and you shall not be nourished, so do not take the time left easy, for the revenge is surely to be taken, and your Lord is waiting for you.

The narrator said: by Allah, I've saw the people at that day puzzled and crying and they've put their hands in their mouths, and I saw an old man standing beside me and crying until his beard became wet and he said: may my father and my mother become ransom for you! Your old men are the best of the old and your youth is the best among the young and your women are best of women, and your lineage is the best of lineage, never to be ashamed.

Then, Fatima Al-Soghrá the daughter of Al-Husayn (PUH) stood up to preach and said: praise be to Allah numbered as much as the sand and the stones, and like the weight of the Throne to the earth, I shall praise Him and believe in Him, and depend on Him, and I shal testify that there is no other god save but Allah, One with no companions, and verily that Mohammed is His slave and His messanger, and that his children were slain on the bank of Al-Forát for no sin or cause. Allahoma, verily I take refuge in You if I was lying about You, or to say something against what You have revealed upon him of covenants for his viceroy `Ali ben Abi Tálib (PUH), the one whose rights were taken and was killed for no crime (like his son was killed yesterday) in a house one of the houses of Allah [meaning the mosque of Kufa where imam `Ali was hit by the sword on his head], while some people claim to be muslims were in it. Woe to their heads! Never defended him against a wrong in his life, nor in his death, until You (Allah) had taken back his soul with good trace, and known faith. Never stepped away to defend Your religion, and You've guided him to be a muslim since his young age, and mentioned his good deeds in his old age. And verily he remained guiding to Your path and to the path of Your prophet until You've taken him back to You, while has disinterested in this life and wishing for the Hereafter, and a fighter for Your path. You've accepted him and chose him and verily You've guided him to the straight path. And then, O people of Kufa, O people of treachery and trickery and the pride! Verily we are a Household that was tested by you, and you were tested by us, and He made our test leading to goodness and made His knowledge and wisdom with us. Thus, we are the owners of His wisdom and the container of His knowledge and wisdom, and His proof in His lands for His bondmen, and verily we've been dignified with His dignity, and we've been preferred by His prophet Mohammed (PUH) over many of His creations in an obvious way, but you've lied to us and made us like the disbelievers, and thought fighting us is allowed and our fortune is to be plundered, like if we were the children of turks or Kabul, like you've killed our grandfather in the yesterday, and your swords are dripping from our blood, the Household, for grudge that was in you since long time. Your eyes were satisfied with that, and your hearts were glad with that, lying about Allah and for a trick that you have made, but Allah is the best who tricks. Verily yourselves would not get scared for the bloodshed you've made within us, and for what your hands have gotten from our fortunes, for the great adversities and troubles were destined in a book before we meet them, and that is easy for Allah, That ye grieve not for the sake of that which hath escaped you, nor yet exult because of that which hath been given. Allah loveth not all prideful boasters. Woe to you! Wait for the damnation and the punishment, it is as if it had befell, and the aversities had been revealed from the sky to destroy you with a punishment, and to make you feel the might of each other, and then all of you shall be in the painful punishment at the judgement day for what you have done to us, verily the damnation of Allah is over the wrong folk. Woe to you! Do you know what hand for you came to stab us? And what soul decided to fight us? Or what leg you've walked with toward us? You've desired to fight us, by Allah, verily your hearts have been harsh, and your livers had been thickened, and your hearings got stamped, and the satan beguiled you and told you what to do, and made a veil over your eyes and you shall never be guided. Woe to you! O people of Kufa, what a hate for the prophet of Allah (PUH) you have, for betraying his brother `Ali ben Abi Tálib (PUH), my grandfather, and the his children and his Household, the purified, and a proud man once said about his pride in that:

Verily we have killed `Ali and the sons of `Ali
with indian swords and with spears
And imprisoned their women like the turks
and struck them and what a struck it was
[indian swords were known for Arabs for the their sharpness and quality]

You've drawn your destiny with your jaws O dishonored sayer!! You've been proud for killing people that Allah had purified and cleansed, so shut up and sit like a dog like your father did!! Every person will get in return what his hands do. Did you envy us? Woe to you! For what Allah preferred us upon you? What is our sin if life got into our raging sea, and your sea is calm and can't cover even a beetle. That is the favor of Allah that is given to anyone He desires, and whoever that Allah had never made a light for him he shall not have a light.

Then the voices raised out loud with cries and weeping, and they said: stop O daughter of the purified, you have burned our hearts and set the fire to our insides. So she went silent.

Then Um-Kalthoom bent `Ali (PUH) preached in that day behind her veil and raised her voice with crying and she said: O people of Kufa, evil to you, why did you let down Husayn and killed him, and plundered his fortunes, and imprisoned his women. Woe to you and may Allah destroy you!! What sin you have commited, and what burden you have taken over your back, and what blood did you shed, and what a dignified woman you've targeted and what children you've plundered and what fortune you have taken. You've killed the best men after the prophet (PUH), and the mercy was taken out from your hearts, and verily the party of Allah shall be the winner, and the party of the devil shall be the loser, and then she said:

You've killed my brother, woe to your mothers
you shall be rewarded with a blazing hell
You've shed bloods that Allah prohibited
and Quran prohibited and then Mohammed

Then the people wept out loud and cried, and the women spread their hairs and put the dust over their heads and scratched their faces and slapped their cheeks and prayed for the woes and punishments. The men also cried, and such numbers of mourners was never seen before.

Then Zaynul-`Abideen [`Ali ben Al-Husayn, 4th imam] made a sign with his hand to make them silence and they went silent, and then stood up, and he praised Allah and blessed the prophet (PUH) and then said: O people, who knew me verily he knew me, and who doesn't know then I shall identify myself for him, I am `Ali ben Al-Husayn ben `Ali ben Abi Tálib (PUH). I am the son of him whose veil was broken and his fortunes were plundered, and his money was taken and his children were imprisoned. I am the son of the one who was slain on the banks of Al-Forát, for no sin or a crime. I am the son of him who was killed and was patient, and that is enough for my pride. O people, I ask you by Allah, do you know that you've written to my father, and then tricked him, and sworn the fealty to him and made the covenant to him and then let him down and killed him?? Woe to you then for what you have done to yourselves, and evil is your thinking! By what eye (look) you shall look at the prophet of Allah?! When he shall say to you: you've killed my Household and broken my veils, then verily you are not from my nation. Then the voices of the people went out loud with cries from all the directions and they said to each other: Verily you are doomed and you don't know, and then he (PUH) said: may the mercy of Allah be upon him who accepts my advice and saved my will for the sake of Allah, and His prophet, and his Household, verily we have a good example in the prophet of Allah.

Then all of them said: we are all, O son of the prophet of Allah, saviors for you and desire no one but you, so command us with your orders may Allah have mercy upon you, for verily we are fighters for those who fight you, and we are peace with whom who make peace with you, and we shall fight Yazeed and make ourselves free from those who wronged you and wronged us. Then he (PUH) said: Allah fobids! O you treacherous, verily there is veil between yourselves and the lusts of yourselves, do you want to come to me like you did with my fathers before?? No, by the God of the dancers (the planets), the wound is not yet cured, my father, may blessings of Allah be upon him, was killed yesterday with his Household, and I didn't forget how bereaved is the prophet of Allah and my father and the children of my father, and his sadness is in my mouth and his bitterness is in my throat and his adversities are running through my chest. My request shall be that you shall not be with us nor against us, and then he (PUH) said:

No wonder Al-Husayn got killed, for his father
was even better than Husayn and more generous
So O people of Kufa don't be happy
for what happened to Husayn for that was more awful
Slain on the banks of the river may my soul be a ransom for him
may the reward of who killed him shall be the hell

Then he said: we've accepted that from you, a head by a head, thus nothing for us and nothing for you (of revenge).

The narrator said: then, Ibn Ziyád sat in the palace and gave a general permission for the people and the head of Al-Husayn was brought and was put before him, so he looked at it and smiled and he had a lash in his hand, so then he began to hit with it the lips of Al-Husayn and say: verily he had a nice looking mouth. Then he said: verily the white hair came so fast to you O Abá `Abdilláh! A day for the day of Badr, and there was in the court Anas ben Málik who cried and said: he (Al-Husayn) is the most like the prophet of Allah (PUH) and verily he was handsome, and beside him there was Zayd ben Arqam, one of the companions of the prophet of Allah and he was an old man, and when he saw that he was hitting his lips he said to him: get your lash away from these two lips, by Allah who there is no other god but Him, verily I saw the prophet kiss these lips so much. Then he started to weep, and Ibn Ziyád said to him: may Allah make your eyes cry, do you cry for the relief of Allah? By Allah, if you were not an old man with senility, I would order for you to be beheaded, so then Zayd ben Arqam got up from the court and said: O people, you are the slaves now after this day, you've killed the son of Fatima and made the son of Morjánah [Ibn Ziyád] a ruler for you, by Allah he shall kill the good of you and make slaves out of your devilish ones, and far may he be who accepts the humiliation. Then he said: O Ibn Ziyád, I shall talk to you such a talk that is harder than this, I've seen the prophet of Allah (PUH) sitting Al-Hasan (PUH) on his right thigh and Husayn (PUH) on his left thigh and then he put his hand on their heads and then said: Allahoma, verily I make them deposits for You and for the rest of the believers. So how was the deposit of the prophet of Allah with you O Ibn Ziyád?

Then, the women of Al-Husayn were entered with the children to the court of Ibn Ziyád, and Zaynab bent `Ali sat in a corner in a disguise, and he asked about her and been told that this is Zaynab the daughter of Fatima, the daughter of the prophet of Allah (PUH), so he came to her and said: praise be to Allah that He defamed you and killed you and showed your lies, and Zaynab then said: praise be to Allah who dignified us with His prophet Mohammed (PUH) and cleansed us, it is but the wrong-doer that shall be defamed and the lies of the unchaste shall be exposed, and we not those. Then Ibn Ziyád said: how do you see the deed of Allah with your brother and his Household?? She replied: I didn't see anything more beautiful, these are people that death was destined upon them and to their graves they went. And verily Allah well make both of you meet each other, and the debate shall go on against you, and wait to see who shall be paralyzed then? May your mother bereave you O son of Morjánah. The narrator said: then Ibn Ziyád went mad and almost got her beaten! But `Amr ben Horayth said to him: she is a woman and the woman is not to be taken for what she says! Then Ibn Ziyád said: Allah had cured my heart from your tyrant, Al-Husayn, and the revolutionists of his Household, and then she said: by my life, you've killed my old man and cut off my branch, and knocked off my roots, and if that is your cure then you had it, and then Ibn Ziyád said: by my life, she's a poet, and her father was too, and then she said: O Ibn Ziyád, what a woman (like me) has to do with poetry, verily I have something that keeps me busy away from poetry, but it is a breath of my chest for what you said.

Then, Ibn Ziyád looked at `Ali ben Al-Husayn and said: who is this? And they told him that this is `Ali ben Al-Husayn, and he said: did not Allah kill `Ali? Then `Ali answered: I had a brother who was called `Ali ben Al-Husayn who was killed by the crowds, he replied: no but Allah killed him, but `Ali (PUH) said: Allah receiveth (men's) souls at the time of their death, and then Ibn Ziyád said: and you dare to reply back? Take him and behead him, and when his aunt Zaynab heard that, she hugged him and said: O Ibn Ziyád, stop from our blood shed for you left no one of us, and if you decided to kill him, then kill me before him, and then Ibn Ziyád looked at her and him for some time and then said: I wonder for such tie of kinship, by Allah, I think she desires to be killed with him, so leave him and I shall decide later.

Then `Ali ben Al-Husayn (PUH) said to his aunt: be silent my aunt until I talk to him, and then he stood before Ibn Ziyád and said: are you threatening me by killing O Ibn Ziyád? Didn't you know martyrdom is a habit of ours and Allah favored that for us, and then Ibn Ziyád ordered to carry `Ali ben Al-Husayn to some room beside the great mosque, and then Zaynab bent `Ali said: no arabian woman shall enter before us, unless she was a maid or a slave, for verily they were taken hostages like us.

Then Ibn Ziyád ordered to take the head of Al-Husayn and tour it around in the roads of Kufa.

Then, Ibn Ziyád went up the pulpit, and praised Allah and said in some of his speech: praise to Allah who showed the truth and its people, and nourished the prince of the believers Yazeed and his party, and killed the liar, the son of the liar and his followers.

While in that situation, `Abdulláh ben `Afeef Al-Azdi stood up, and he was one of the shiites and a great worshipper, and his left eye was gone in the battle of Jamal [battle of imam `Ali and `Á'ishah, the wife of the prophet, after which, imam `Ali won], and his right eye was gone at the day of Siffeen [a battle of imam `Ali and Mo`áwiyah the father of Yazeed, after which imam `Ali won], and he used to remain in the great mosque and pray there until night time, so he said: O son of Morjánah, verily the liar is you and your father, and the one who used you and his father O enemy of Allah! Do you kill the children of the prophets and talk with such a speech on the pulpits of the muslims?? Then Ibn Ziyád got angry and said: who is that talking to me? He replied: I am the one who talks O enemy of Allah! Do you kill the purified Household which Allah cleansed and made clean, and claim that you are a muslim, Alas! Any helper! Where are the sons of Mohájireen and Ansár? [Mohájireen: immigrants from Mecca to Medina, Ansár: inhabitants of Medina who nourished the prophet when he immigrated], they should take the revenge from you and from your tyrant, the damned the son of the damned, who was damned by the prophet Mohammed (PUH).

He said (the narrator): the anger of Ibn Ziyád increased until his veins blowed up and said: get him! And the soldiers came from all directions to take him, but the nobles of the tribe of Azd of his cousins stood up and freed him from the soldiers, and got him out from the mosque's door and took him back to his house, and then Ibn Ziyád said: go to that blind man, the blind man of Azd, may Allah make his heart blind as well, and get him for me.

So they went to him, and when Azd tribe knew about that they gathered with the tribes of Yemen to protect their man, and Ibn Ziyád got the tidings about that and he gathered the tribes of Modhar under Mohammed ben Al-Ash`ath, and he ordered him to fight the people, and they fought against each other severely, until a group of Arabs got killed, and the fellows of Ibn Ziyád reached the house of `Abdulláh ben `Afeef, and they broke the door and got into the house, and his daughter shouted: the people came from where you were afraid! He said: don't be afraid, get me the sword, and so she did and he started to defend himself. Then he daughter said: O father how I wish that I was a man to fight before you against those wicked men, the killers of the purified Household.

The people started to rotate around him from all directions, while he was defending himself, and no one could get him, and whenever they come to him from one direction, she (his daughter) would say: O father they're coming from that direction, until they out numbered him and surrounded him, and his daughter then said: Alas! What humiliation! My father is surrounded and he has no one to nourish him, so he started to rotate his sword and say:

I swear if my eyes only can see
then you would have no way to me

And they kept on like that until they got him, and then he was carried and got into the court of Ibn Ziyád, and when he saw him he said: praise to Allah who disappointed you! `Abdulláh ben `Afeef said then: O enemy of Allah by what did He disappoint me? Then Ibn Ziyád said: O enemy of Allah, what do you say about `Uthmán ben `Affán [3rd caliph]? He replied: O slave of Bani `Iláj, O son of Morjánah, and he cursed him and said:

what is the matter between you and `Uthmán?? whether he sinned or made a favor, and whether he made good or bad, verily Allah is the Carer for His creation, and He shall judge among them and `Uthmán with just and truth. But ask me about your father and you, and about Yazeed and his father? Then Ibn Ziyád said: by Allah I shall not ask you about anything else, and you shall taste death severely!

Then, `Abdulláh ben `Afeef said: praise to Allah the God of the creations, verily I was asking Allah to make me a martyr before your mother delivered you, and I asked Allah to make that by the most evil creature and the most behated one by Him, and when my sightness was taken away I was despaired of being a martyr, and now - praise to Allah - who made me have it after being despaired about it, and made me know the answer of my old pray, so then Ibn Ziyád said: behead him, and so they did and he was crucified in the moorland.

The narrator said: and `Ubaydilláh ben Ziyád wrote a letter to Yazeed ben Mo`áwiyah telling him about the killing of Al-Huysan (PUH) with his Household, and when the letter reached Yazeed, he replied back ordering him to bring the head of Al-Husayn and the heads of those who got killed him with him, with the children and the women.

Ibn Al-Jawzi [a historian] said: and the people toured them, and whenever they would settle down in some place they would take the head out from a chest that was made for it, and put it on a spear and guard him all night until the time of moving, and then they return it back to the chest and move, and they settled in some places, and in one of these places there was an abbey with a monk, so they took the head from the chest as usual and put it on a spear and got it guarded, and they supported the spear with the abbey of the christian man, and when it was midnight, the monk saw a light from the place of the head to the sky, so he went to the people and said: who are you? They said: we are the fellows of Ibn Ziyád, then he said: whose head is this? They replied: this is the head of Al-Husayn ben `Ali ben Abi Tálib, the son of Fatima the daughter of the prophet, he said: this is the head of the son of the daughter of your own prophet?! They said: yes, he said: evil people are you! If the Messiah had a son we would make our eyes a home for him, and then he said: do you accept some deal? They said: and what is that? He said: I have 10 thousands Dirham [currency of that time], you shall take it and give me the head to be with me this night and when you want to leave you shall take it back? They said: no harm with that!

So, they gave him the head and he gave them the money, and the monk took the head and washed it and put perfumes on it and left it with him, and put it on his thigh, and cried all night, and when the morning appeared, he said: O head, I have nothing but myself, and verily I testify that there is no other god but Allah, and your grandfather Mohammed is the messenger of Allah, and I testify that I am one of your followers. Then he left the abbey and worked on serving the Household (PUT).

Then the people toured with the head of Al-Husayn and the heads of his Household, with the prisoners of women and children, and when they were close to Damascus, Um-Kalthoom got closer to Shimr who was among them and said to him: I have a request for you!! He said: and what is your request of daughter of `Ali?? She said: if you got into the town then take us in such a road that has less people, and tell them to get the heads out and away from us, for verily we've been ashamed for how much they looked at us and we are in such condition, so he ordered to answer her request and to put the heads on the spears among the prisoners as to oppose her request and he took a road with lot of people until they reached the gate of

Damascus, and then an old man came and got closer to the women of Al-Husayn (PUH) and said: praise be to Allah who killed you and destroyed you and made a relief for the lands from your men and helped the prince of the believers Yazeed against you!

Then `Ali ben Al-Husayn said: O old man, did you read Quran? He replied: yes. Then he said: did you know this phrase "I ask of you no fee therefor, save lovingkindness among kinsfolk"? The old man replied: yes, I read that. Then `Ali (PUH) said: then we are the kinsfolk O old man. Then, did you read in chapter of Bani Israel [The Israelites, chapter 17 of Quran] "Give the kinsman his due" ?? Then the old man replied: yes I did read that. Then `Ali ben Al-Husayn said: then verily we are the kinsmen O old man. Did you read "And know that whatever ye take as spoils, lo! a fifth thereof is for Allah, and for the messenger and for the kinsman..."? The man replied: yes. Then `Ali ben Al-Husayn said: we are the kinsmen. Did you read "Allah's wish is but to remove uncleanness far from you, O Folk of the Household, and cleanse you with a thorough cleansing"? The old man said: I read that. Then `Ali (PUH) said: we are the Household that was mentioned in the phrase of purification. Then the old man remained regret for what he said, and then looked at Zaynul-`Abideen (`Ali ben Al-Husayn) and said: by Allah, you are them??

The imam said: we are verily them with no doubt, by the rights of our grandfather the messenger of Allah verily we are them, and then the old man started to cry and he threw his turban away and raised his head to the sky and said: Allahoma verily we make ourselves free from the enemy of the Household of Mohammed, whether it was a human or Djinn. Then he said: is there a way to repent? He (`Ali) replied: yes, if you repented, then Allah shall forgive you and you are with us! He said: I am repenting. The tidings of the old man then reached Yazeed ben Mo`áwiyah, and he ordered for him to be killed.

Sahl ben Sa`d Al-Sá`idi said: I was out for the holy house (in Jerusalem) and when I reached the middle of Shám [Damascus], I found out a city with rivers going through it and many trees and the curtains were hanged and the people were happy and their women played the tambourines and the drums. So I said to myself: there is no single festival for the people of Damascus that we don't know. Then, I saw some people talking to each other so I said: O people, do you have in Damascus a festival that we don't know?? They replied: O old man, verily we see you a nomad and a stranger (from here), so I said: I am Sahl ben Sa`d, and I've seen the prophet of Allah (PUH), they replied: O Sahl, you don't wonder for the sky that it doesn't rain blood and the earth doesn't sink with its people?!! I said: and why is that?! They replied: this is the head of Al-Husayn, the Household of Mohammed (PUH) is being driven from the lands of Iraq!! I said: Alas! what a wonder! The head of Al-Husayn is being gifted and the people are happy? I asked then: from what gate shall they pass? And they pointed out to a gate that is called Bábul-Sá`át [The gate (door) of hours, so called for the many hours that the Household spent there many hours to get into the court of Yazeed]. And in that situation, I saw the banners follow each other, and then I saw a knight with a flag that has no top and on the top of it was there a head that looked almost similar to the face of the prophet of Allah (PUH). Then after that I saw women riding camels with no saddles, so I got closer to one of their children and said: O maid, who are you? She said: I am Sokaynah the daughter of Al-Husayn. Then I said to her: do you need anything? I am Sahl ben Sa`d, one of those who saw your grandfather the prophet of Allah (PUH) and heard his speech. She said: O Sahl, tell the carrier of the head to put the head in front of us, so the people would get busy looking at it instead of looking at the daughters of the prophet of Allah (PUH).

He said: then I got closer to the carrier and said to him: would you do me a favor for 400 dinars? He said: and what is that? I said then: make the head in front of the harem, and so he did and I paid him what I've promised.

Al-Zohari said: and when the heads arrived, and Yazeed at that time was on a watch-tower over Jayroon, and he heard a crow's sound, and said to himself:

When those carried ones appeared and raised
those suns on the hills of Jayroon
The crow cried so I said be right or not
for verily I've got my debts from my opponent

Then, the Household of Al-Husayn and the women were entered to the court of Yazeed ben Mo`áwiyah and they were tied with robes, and when they all got in there, and in that situation, `Ali ben Al-Husayn (PUH) said: by Allah O Yazeed, what do you think the prophet of Allah would say if he saw us in this situation?

Then Yazeed ordered to cut off the robes and he asked for a file and started to file the cuffs that were on the neck of imam Zaynul-`Ábideen [`Ali ben Al-Husayn] (PUH).

When they removed the cuffs from his neck, the blood gushed out from his neck. Ibn Al-Atheer [a historian] said in his book Al-Kámil: and a syrian man (who was in the court) looked at Fatima the daughter Al-Huysan and said to Yazeed: give me this maid, and Fatima said (later on): at that time I got shocked and I thought this is allowed for them, and I took the clothes of my aunt Zaynab and said: Alas! my aunt! I was made an orphan and now to be used?? Then Zaynab said: no, and this wicked has no dignity. She knew that this will never happen, so she looked to the syrian man and said: by Allah you've lied and been wicked, and by Allah this is not to be for you or for him [meaning Yazeed]. Then Yazeed got angry and said: by Allah you've lied, I am able to do so if I wanted to!!

She said: no by Allah, Allah did not make that for you unless you've been out from this religion, and then Yazeed got angry even more and said: do you talk to me in that way? Verily who got out from this religion is your father and your brother, and Zaynab said: by the religion of Allah, and the religion of my father, and the religion of my brother, you've been guided with your grandfather and your father, if you were a muslim!!

He said: you've lied O enemy of Allah, and she replied: you are a prince that curse with unjust and succeed with your might, then as if he was embarrassed and went silent.

Then the syrian man got back again to his request and Yazeed then said to him: stop it, may Allah give you a mortal fate. Then the syrian man asked: who is this maid? Yazeed said: this is Fatima the daughter of Al-Huysan and that is Zaynab the daughter of `Ali ben Abi Tálib (PUH). The syrian man then said: Al-Husayn the son of Fatima? And `Ali ben Abi Tálib?!! He replied: yes, and then the syrian man said: may Allah damn you O yazeed, do you kill the Household of your prophet and imprison their children, by Allah I thought they are from the romans, then Yazeed said: by Allah I shall make you follow them, and then he ordered to behead him.

Then Yazeed ordered to bring the head of Al-Husayn, and he put it in front of him in a tub made of gold, and the women were behind him, then Sokaynah and Fatima tried to get a sight of the head and Yazeed was covering it away from them, and when they saw it they shouted out loud and cried.

Then Yazeed gave a general permission for the people to come into the court, and Yazeed took his rod and started to hit the lips of Al-Husayn and say: a day for the day of Badr, and then said:

Our people denied to be just with us
so rods in our faith full of blood were just
Courage of men that were mighty for us
was shut off and they were the most unjust

Then, Yahyá ben Al-Hakam -the brother of Marwán- who was sitting there said:

Verily, the head beside the river's bank is more close in relation
rather than Ibn Ziyád, the slave of the dirty lineage
Somayyah now is has a lineage in many numbers
and today the Household of the Chosen has no lineage

Then Yazeed struck him on his chest and said: shut up, may you have no mother.

And as for Zaynab, when she saw the head of her brother, she took her pocket and torn it and then called with a sad voice that shaked the hearts: Alas! Husayn! O beloved of the prophet, O son of Mecca and Miná [a village around Mecca], O son of Fatima Al-Zahrá'.

Then Yazeed started to sing and say:

Wish if my ancestors in Badr testified
the fear of Khazraj from the swords' beats
Verily they would be glad and happy
then say O Yazeed don't ever stop
We've killed the bravest of their masters
and made it equal to Badr's day and it was

Verily I am not from the tribe of Khondof
if I didn't take revenge from Ahmad for what he did
Háshim played with the throne and thus,
no tidings were brought and nor inspiration
[Ahmad is another version of Mohammed]

And while he was singing this poem, suddenly the voice of Zaynab shocked his hearings, for she didn't see anyone who would answer Yazeed ben Mo`áwiyah, so she stood up and said: praise to Allah the God of the worlds, and blessings of Allah on His prophet and his Household. Truely Allah had said: Then evil was the consequence to those who dealt in evil, because they denied the revelations of Allah and made a mock of them. O Yazeed, did you think, when you've turned the corners of the earth and the horizons of the sky over us and made hostages driven like the prisoners of war, did you think that we are behated by Allah and He liked you, and that was for how dangerous you are in His eyes, so you raised your nose and looked at the tip of your cloak (with pride) in happiness, when you saw the life is assured for you and the matters are done good for you, and when our fortune and might been away from your way. Just wait, did you forget Allah's saying: And let not those who disbelieve imagine that the rein We give them bodeth good unto their souls. We only give them rein that they may grow in sinfulness. And theirs will be a shameful doom. Is it fair O son of Tolaqá' [Tolaqá' : freed men, a group of men got captured in the day of Badr and the prophet released them, and Yazeed's ancestors were among them], is it fair that you put your harem behind the veils while you drive the daughters of the prophet like prisoners, and you've broken their veils and showed their faces, and the enemies got them toured from one town to another, and people talk about them, while their faces are looked at by the near and the far, and the mean and the noble, with no man from their household, and no protector.

How it is possible to look at him who chewed the livers of the faithful and his meat grown up with the blood of the martyrs? And how is it possible that he wouldn't hate us severely, the Household, who looked at us with the eyes of envy and hatred, and then you say as easy as it could be:

Verily they would be glad and happy
then say O Yazeed don't ever stop

while you bend on the lips of Abá `Abdilláh, the lord of youth of paradise, and you hit it with your rod. How come you don't say that? And you've severed the wound and knocked off the origins by shedding the bloods of the Household of Mohammed (PUH), and the stars of earth, from the Household of `Abdul-Mottalib [the grandfather of the prophet], and you call your ancestors as if you were calling them, and verily you shall follow them soon, and then you will wish if you've been paralyzed and muted, and never said what you've said and never did what you've done. Allahoma, take our rights, and take revenge from those who wronged us, and let Your wrath befall upon those who shed our bloods and killed our protectors. By Allah, you've severed your skin only, and you've cut your own meat, and you shall meet the prophet of Allah (PUH) with what you've put on your back of the blood of his Household and of what veils you've broken for his daughters, after Allah gathers them all together and take their rights. Think not of those, who are slain in the way of Allah, as dead. Nay, they are living. With their Lord they have provision, and Allah is enough Judge, and Mohammed (PUH) is enough for an opponent, and Gabriel is enough for being a support, and he who advised you with evil and made you rule of the muslims' necks how evil is to be for the wrong-doers and whoever shall be in an evil place and with the weakest army. And though destiny made me talk to you, verily I see you small in my eyes and not worthy even to my rebuke, but the eyes are full of tears and the chests are full of agony. Alas! What a wonder for killing the party of Allah the Chosen, by the party of satan the free, and these are the hands, they are dropping from our bloods, and these are the mouths, they are getting from our meats, and these are the purified corpses, they are visited by the wolves and hyenas, and if you stood against us you shall find us a fierce enemy, at a time when you only see what you've done by your own hands, and verily your God is not an unjust for His bondmen. Thus, to Allah shall be the complaint, and He shall help. Then, trick your tricks, and walk along your path, and do your best, by Allah you shall never erase our mention, and never kill our inspiration, and never reach our level, and its shame shall never leave you, and what is your opinion but to doom? And what are your days but numbers? And what are your gatherings (men) but to be separated? At the day when the caller shall call and say: may the damnation of Allah befall upon the wrong-doers. Then praise to Allah the Lord of the worlds who judged for our first with happiness and forgiveness, and to our last with martyrdom and mercy, and we shall ask Allah to complete their rewards and add more for them, and make it easy for us verily He is Merciful and Beloved, and Allah is our Judge and He is Dependable.

Then Yazeed said:

O cry that praise the criers
death is easy for the mourners

Then, a christian man who was a messenger from caesar to Yazeed looked around and said: we have in some islands, the trace of the hoof of the donkey that Jesus used to ride and we make pilgrimage there every year from all around the lands and the vows are made there, and we glorify it like you glorify your own books, and verily I testify that you are wrong-doers.

Then Yazeed got angry for this saying and ordered to kill him, so he stood up and went to the head and kissed it and said the two testimonies [the two testimonies required to enter into Islam].

Then Yazeed took our the head from the court and hanged it on the gate of the palace for 3 days, and when Hind bent `Amr, Yazeed's wife, heard about that, she went to him uncovering her head with bare feet and with no veils, to the court of Yazeed, and she said: O Yazeed, the head of the son of the daughter of the prophet is on our gate? Then Yazeed went to her and covered her and said to her: O Hind, he is the scream of the hashimites!! Ibn Ziyád just got him.

Then Yazeed ben Mo`áwiyah went to the mosque and ordered the preacher to go up the pulpit and curse `Ali and Al-Husayn while `Ali ben Al-Husayn was attendant, and the preacher did that, and then `Ali ben Al-Husayn: woe to you O preacher! you've bought the satisfaction of the created with the wrath of the Creator, so prepare your seat that is made of fire.

Then, `Ali ben Al-Husayn said to Yazeed: do you allow me to go up those sticks (the pulpit) and talk some words that gets the satisfaction of Allah and for these people the rewards? But Yazeed denied to allow him, and the people said then: allow him to go on the pulpit so that we may hear something from him, and he replied: if he went up there he wouldn't come down unless with my defame and the defame of Abu-Sufyán's household!! They said: and what can this kid say? He said: he is from a household that was given the wisdom!! But they insisted and insisted until he allowed him to go up the pulpit, so then he (`Ali ben Al-Husayn) praised Allah and blessed the prophet of Allah, and he said a speech that made the eyes go on with tears and filled the hearts with fear, and he said: O people, I warn you against this life and what is in it, for it is a vanishing place and a moving one, that moves with its people from one situation to another. Verily, the passing old centuries have vanished the old nations who were longer in lives more than you and made more traces than you did; they were all vanished by the hands of time, and conquered by the snakes and the worms, all of them were destroyed by this life like if they were not its people. The dust have eaten their meat, and removed their beauty and wasted their organs and changed their colors, and they were grinded by the hands of time. Do you wish to live after them? Allah forbids!! Verily you shall follow them, so chase after what is left of your ages with the good deeds, like I can see you moving from your palaces to your graves filled with unhappiness, and how many by Allah there was a dead man that got his regret in complete, when there is no help for those who regret and those who wrong. They found what they did, and what they had was presented, and what they did was in front of their eyes and your Lord do not wrong anyone. They are verily in the homes of the adversities sleeping, and in the camps of the deads are laying, and waiting for the cry of the judgement day, and the falling of the great events day "that He may reward those who do evil with that which they have done, and reward those who do good with goodness."

Then he said: O people, we are given six and preferred by seven: we are given the wisdom and clemency and forgiveness and eloquence and bravery and the love in the hearts of the believers. And we are preferred by: from us the prophet of Allah, and from us the Righteous [imam `Ali] and Al-Tayyár [Tayyár: the flying man, a title for Ja`far the brother of imam `Ali, because he lost his both hands in war], and from us the lion of Allah and His prophet [Hamzah the prophet's uncle], and from us the two septs of this nation [the grandsons of the prophet], and from us shall be the Guider of this nation [imam Al-Mahdi, the last imam for twelvers shiites].

Who knew me then he knew me, and who did not know me then I shall tell him my lineage and ancestry: O people, I am the son of Mecca and Miná, I am the son of Zamzam and Safá [Zamzam is a spring in Mecca and Safá is a mountain there], I am the son of him who took the Zakat by the edges of his cloak, I am the son of the best man who wore clothes, I am the son of the best man who wore sandals and walked with bare feet, I am the son of the best man who toured and walked (in pilgrimage), I am the son of the best man who did pilgrimage, I am the son of him who was carried by Al-Boráq in the air [Al-Boráq: a creature that carried the prophet in his ascending to heavens], I am the son of him who was carried by night from the Holy Mosque (Mecca) to the Aqsá mosque (Jerusalem), I am the son of him who Gabriel carried him to lote-tree of the utmost boundary, I am the son of him who drew nigh and came down till he was (distant) two bows' length or even nearer, I am the son of him who prayed with the angels of heaven two bows, I am the son of him who got the inspiration of The Glorified, I am the son of Mohammed the Chosen.

I am the son of `Ali Al-Mortadhá, I am the son of him who struck the noses of the creations until they said no other god save but Allah, I am the son of him who struck with two swords before the prophet of Allah, and stabbed with two spears, and immigrated the two immigrations, and sworn fealty for two times, and fought in Badr and Hunayn, and never disbelieved in Allah for a blink of an eye.

I am the son of the best of the faithful men, and the heir of the prophets, and the fighter of the disbelievers, and the bee of the believers, and the light of the Mojáhideen (fighters), and the crown of the criers and the best of the worshippers and the most patient one, and the best of prayers from the Household of Táhá and Yaseen, that is the prophet of the Lord of the worlds.

I am the son of him who is supported by Gabriel, that is nourished by Michael, I am the son of him the protector of the muslims, and the killer of the heretics and those who break the oaths and the unjust, and the fighter for those who took his rights by force, and the most proud one who walked from the whole of Qoraysh, and the first one to answer Allah and His prophet from the believers, and the first one (in worshipping), and the breaker of the aggressors, and the terminator of the disbelievers, and the arrow of Allah against the hypocrites, and the tongue of wisdom of the worshippers, and the nourisher of the religion of Allah and the viceroy of the commands of Allah, and the garden of wisdom of Allah and the holder of His sciences (wisdoms).

Forgiver and with bright face, gatherer of goodness and purified, mighty and satisfied, brave with courage, patient and fasting, the cutter of the lineages and the terminator of the parties (of the disbelievers).

The most brave, and with the firmest feet, and with the strongest will and with the hardest power, a brave lion, that grinds them in the war when the swords are raised and the reins are close, a grinding like the stone mill and threw them away like the winds do to the grains, the lion of Hijáz, and the ram of Iraq.

From Mecca and Medina, fought in Badr and Uhud, an immigrant (to Medina), from Arabs he is their master and in the war he is the lion, and the father of the two septs (grandsons), Al-Hasan and Al-Husayn, that is my grandfather `Ali ben Abi Tálib.

Then he said: I am the son of Fatima Al-Zahrá', I am the son of the lady of the women, I am the son of Khadeejah Al-Kobrá [the prophet's wife].

I am the son of him who was killed with unjust
I am the son of him whose head was cut from its back
I am the son of him who died of thirst
I am the son of him who was laid down in Karbala
I am the son of him whose cloak and turban were stolen
I am the son of him whom the angels of heaven cried upon
I am the son of him whom the djinn cried upon on earth and the birds as well in air
I am the son of him whose head is presented on the tops of spears
I am the son of him whose harem are toured from Iraq to Damascus

So he kept saying I am, I am, until the people went on crying and weeping and Yazeed afraid that will lead to riot so he ordered the caller for the prayer to call. Thus, when the caller said: Allahu Akbar [Allah is Greater], `Ali ben Al-Husayn said: nothing is greater than Allah, you've made great a Great One who is not to be measured. When the caller said: Ash-hado an lá iláha illá Allah [verily I testify there is no other god but Allah], `Ali ben Al-Husayn then said: my hair and my skin and my bones and meat and my blood all testified with it. When the caller said: Ash-hado anna Mohammadan rasool Allah [verily I testify that Mohammed is the prophet of Allah], here he looked from the pulpit to Yazeed and said: this Mohammed, is he my or your grandfather O Yazeed? If you claimed he is your grandfather then verily you've lied, and if you said he is my grandfather then why did you kill his Household?

Then Zaynul-`Ábideen got down from the pulpit, and all of those who were in the mosque departed and gathered around Zaynul-`Ábideen.

Then, when Yazeed got afraid of the riot and the reversal of the matter, he ordered to fasten the exit of imam Zaynul-`Ábideen and the children from Damascus to their homeland and did what they wanted, and ordered Al-No`mán ben Basheer and other folks to go along with them to Medina with easiness.

When Zaynul-`Ábideen knew about the acceptance of Yazeed, he asked from Yazeed to give him back all of the heads to bury them in their own places, and Yazeed didn't dare to refuse, so he gave him back the head of Al-Husayn with the rest of the heads of his Household and companions, and he buried them with the bodies (as it is mentioned in the book of Habeeb Al-Siyar).

The narrator said: and when they went out of Damascus to Medina, they made their way passing through the lands of Iraq, and when they got closer, they said to the guide: pass us through to the land of Karbala.

When they reached the location, they found Jábir ben `Abdulláh Al-Ansári and some folk from the hashimite, and some men from the Household of the prophet and they all came to visit the grave of Al-Husayn (PUH), and they all came at one time and the met each other the cries and weeping and slapping the faces and they made a mourning for some days.

As reported from `Atiyyah Al-`Oofi that he said: I went out with Jábir ben `Abdulláh Al-Ansári to visit the grave of Al-Husayn (PUH), and when we arrived at Karbala, Jábir went to the bank of Al-Forát and made a wash and then wear a cloth around his waist, and wore another cloth, and then opened a pocket with some perfume and got some of it on his body, and then he walked to the holy grave with bare feet, and didn't step one step without mentioning the name of Allah, and when he reached the grave he said: make me touch it [he was a blind man]. `Atiyyah said: then I made him touch the grave, and then he fell down on the grave and went in a coma, so I sprankled some water on him, and when he woke up, he said: O Husayn - three times- and then said: a beloved one that doesn't answer his lover!! Then he said: and how shall you answer?? With your blood of the neck dropping down on your back, and your head was separated from your body. Verily I testify that you are the son of the best of the prophets, and the son of the master of viceroys, and the son of him who is the ally to faithfulness and the son of the guidance, and the fifth of the people of the cover (cloak) [the story of the cover, a story in which the prophet Mohammed gathered his daughter and `Ali and their sons under one cloak and he was one of them and the prophet prayed for them], and the son of the master of the virtuous and the son of Fatima the lady of the women.

Why you shouldn't be like this? While you were feeded by the master of the prophets and grown in the laps of the virtuous, and sucked from the breast of faith, and weaned by Islam.

So, purified you are alive and purified you are in death, but the hearts of the believers are not good about your death, and not doubtful about your living. Thus, may the peace of Allah and His blessings be upon you, and I testify that you've gone on the path of your brother, Yahyá ben Zakariyyá [John the son of Zachary, Zacharias].

Then he looked around the grave and said: peace upon you O souls that gathered around Al-Husayn (PUH) and settled in his place. Verily I testify that you've done the prayers, and gave the

Zakat, and ordered with goodness and prohibited the evil (deeds) and fought against the disbelievers and worshipped Allah until the truth had been showed for you. By Him who sent Mohammed (PUH) with the truth, we've been with you in what you've been through.

`Atiyyah said: then I said to Jábir: and how is that? and we didn't go into a single valley, and didn't go on the top of a single mountain, and we didn't hit with a single sword, and the people had their heads separated from their bodies and the children were made orphans and their wives were made widows?? Then he said to me: O `Atiyyah, I've heard my beloved the prophet of Allah (PUH) saying once: he who loved some people he shall be gathered with them, and he who loved the deeds of some people he shall be gathered with them. By Him who sent Mohammed (PUH) with the truth, my will and the wills of my companions was to go after what Al-Husayn was after with his companions.

`Atiyyah said: and while we were talking in that situation, we saw blackness that arrived at us from the direction of Damascus, and then I said: O Jábir, I see a great blackness that is coming to us from Damascus, then Jábir looked to his slave and said to him: go and see what is this blackness? If they were the fellows of `Ubaydilláh ben Ziyád then get back to us so that we may find a shelter, and if that was my lord and master Zaynul-`Ábideen then you are free for the sake of Allah.

Then the slave went and came back in a hurry and slapping his slave and say: stand up O Jábir and receive the harem of the prophet of Allah, this is my master and my lord `Ali ben Al-Husayn (PUH) had arrived with his aunts and his sisters, then Jábir stood up and walked with bare feet and uncovering his head and got closer to Zaynul-`Ábideen, and the imam said: are you Jábir? He replied: yes, O son of the prophet of Allah. Then he said: O Jábir, verily here our men were killed, and our children were slain, and our women were taken prisoners and our tents were burnt. And like I can hear Zaynab saying:

O settlers in Karbala do you have the tidings
about our dead people and what are their banners
What is the condition of a corpse of a dead man in your lands
that remained for three days with no single visitor
By Allah have you buried it in the ground
and did its remains got into the grave?

Then she went to the grave of her brother Abá `Abdilláh Al-Husayn (PUH) weeping and crying, while the daughters of the prophet were moving from the grave of Abá `Abdilláh to the grave of Abul-Fadhl Al-`Abbás (PUH).

Then the household remained for 3 days in the land Karbala, and after that they headed to Medina. And when they got closer to Medina, they settled down there and imam Zaynul-`Ábideen looked at Bishr ben Haðlam and said to him: O Bishr, may Allah have mercy upon your father, verily he was a poet, so are you able to say some? He replied: yes O son of the prophet of Allah, I am verily a poet, and he (PUH) said: then go to Medina and mourn Abá `Abdilláh Al-Husayn.

Bishr said: then I tode my horse, and ran until I got into Medina, and when I reached the mosque of the prophet of Allah, I raised my voice with weeping and said:

O people of Yathrib [Medina] no settling for you in it
Al-Husayn had been killed so cry in abundance
The body is in Karbala covered with blood
and his head on the spears go on circles

Then I said: O people of Medina, this is `Ali ben Al-Husayn with his aunts and sisters got into your vicinity and settled down in your space and I am his messenger to you to let you know his place.

He (Bishr) said: and no single noble woman stayed in her home, and all of them went out slapping their faces and praying for the punishment, and I've seen criers as much as it was in that day, and no bitter day more than that day after the death of the prophet (PUH), and I heard a maid crying for Al-Husayn and say:

Mourner mourned my master and hurt me
and made me sick a moruner who mourned him and shocked me
Thus, my eyes, cry a lot and pour the tears
and be generous with the tears after your tears altogether
Over the son of the prophet of Allah and the son of his viceroy
though even he is far in lands that are far away from us

Then she said: O mourner, you've renewed our sadness about Abá `Abdilláh (PUH) and hurt our wounds that were never healed, so who are you may Allah have mercy upon you, so I said: I am Bishr ben Halðam, came from my lord `Ali ben Al-Husayn (PUH) and he settled down in that location, with the children of Abá `Abdilláh Al-Husayn (PUH) and his women. He continued: then they left me and went to meet him so I struck my horse to get back to them, and I've found the people taken seats along the roads and the streets, so I got down from my horse and passed through the necks of people until I got closer to the tent and `Ali ben Al-Husayn was inside, then he went out holding a kerchief wiping his tears, and behind him was his servant with a chair. So, he put it down for him, and he sat down and couldn't hold his tears, and the people raised their voices with tears and cries and gave solace from every corner, and that spot got condensed with the noise, and then he signed with his hand to let them go silence, and so they did, then he said: Praise be to Allah, Lord of the Worlds, Master of the Day of Judgment, the Initiator of the whole creations, who got far and raised up in high heavens, and got closer and knew the secrets, we shall praise Him for the great adversities and the troubles of time, and pains of disasters and for the bitterness of matters and the greatness of the troubles. O people, verily Allah had - and praise to Him- tested us with great troubles, and a hole in Islam that is great, Abá `Abdilláh was killed with his Household, and his women were imprisoned with his children, and his head was toured around the lands over the pikes, and this is the trouble that nothing is like it. O people, who of your men will be glad after killing him, or what heart shall not be sad for him, or what eye shall keep the tear from falling?? Verily, the seven heavens cried for his death, and seas cried with its waves, and the heavens with its corners, and the earth with its lands, and the trees with its branches, and the whales in the depth of the sea, and the closer angels, and the rest of the folks of heavens. O people, what heart wouldn't be broken for his death? Or what heart doesn't miss him, or what hearing that doesn't go deaf after hearing about such hole in Islam? O people, we've became banished and scattered in all lands like the children of turks or Kabul, for no crime we did, and no mistake we committed and no change in laws of Islam we did, and we've never heard about such a thing amont our ancestors, verily this is only an innovation. By Allah, if the prophet of Allah (PUH) went to fight them as much as he advised them about us, they wouldn't do much more than this. Verily we are to Allah and we shall be back to Him. What a great adversity, and what painful one is it, and what a horrible one is it, and we shall depend on Allah for what befell us, verily He is Great and a revenge Taker.

Then Zaynul-`Abideen went to Medina and found it like ghosts town and its people mourning, and found the houses of his family empty, and mourning about its inhabitants.

As for the daughters of the prophet (PUH), they went to the house of Abá `Abdilláh Al-Husayn (PUH). Then Um-Kalthoom called and said:

City of our grandfather don't accept us
verily we came with sadness and losses
We've been out from you in numbers
and came back with no men or sons

www.ingramcontent.com/pod-product-compliance
Lightning Source LLC
Chambersburg PA
CBHW051606010526
44119CB00056B/798